Hooked on Java™

Creating Hot Web Sites with Java Applets

Arthur van Hoff, Sami Shaio,
and Orca Starbuck
Sun Microsystems, Inc.

Addison-Wesley Publishing Company

Reading, Massachusetts • Menlo Park, California • New York
Don Mills, Ontario • Wokingham, England • Amsterdam
Bonn • Sydney • Singapore • Tokyo • Madrid • San Juan
Paris • Seoul • Milan • Mexico City • Taipei

Library of Congress Cataloging-in-Publication Data

van Hoff, Arthur.
  Hooked on Java: creating hot Web sites with Java applets / Arthur van Hoff, Sami Shaio, and Orca Starbuck.
    p. cm.
  Includes index.
  ISBN 0-201-48837-X
  1. Object-oriented programming (Computer science) 2. Java (Computer program language) 3. Multimedia systems. 4. World-Wide Web (Information retrieval system) I. Shaio, Sami. II. Starbuck, Orca. III. Title.
QA76.64.V36 1996   95–43866
005.75—dc20   CIP

Sponsoring Editor: Kim Fryer
Project Manager: Sarah Weaver
Production Coordinator: Erin Sweeney
Cover design: Robert Dietz
Text design: Kim Arney

4 5 6 7 8 9-MA-0099989796
Fourth printing, February 1996

Addison-Wesley books are available for bulk purchases by corporations, institutions, and other organizations. For more information please contact the Corporate, Government, and Special Sales Department at (800) 238-9682.

Find A-W Developers Press on the World-Wide Web at:
http://www.aw.com/devpress/

To Marleen and Trix—*Arthur van Hoff*

For Mireille, Soli, and Jack—*Sami Shaio*

To my husband, Benjamin—*Orca Starbuck*

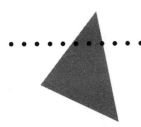

Contents

List of Figures

Acknowledgments

We'd like to thank Marc Andreessen, James Gosling, Bill Joy, Eric Schmidt, Ruth Hennigar, Keith Wollman, Kim Fryer, the Java team, and all the applet writers for making this book possible.

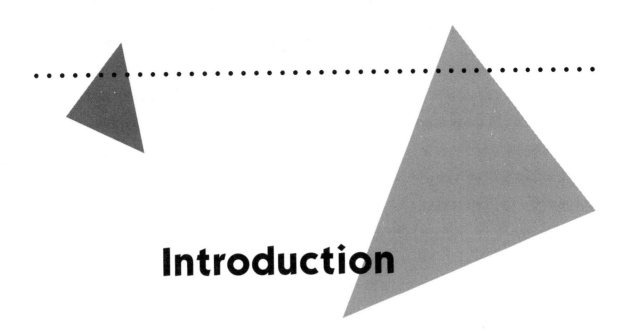

Introduction

If you want to learn what Java applets are and how to use them to bring your World-Wide Web site to life, this is the book for you. In these pages we'll describe many Java applets, and you'll learn how to add them to your Web page without programming. We'll also explain how these applets work. For the adventurous, we'll show you how to write your own Java applets.

The Java applets described in this book, which are also on the CD-ROM, will run in any Java-compatible browser on any computer. This means that the applets will work just as well in Netscape Navigator on Microsoft Windows 95 as they do in HotJava on Sun Microsystem's Solaris. Actually, this is one of the reasons why Java is so powerful: it will work on any computer. But more about that later.

Who This Book Is for

▶ Webmasters and information content providers on the World-Wide Web who want to create more exciting Web pages
▶ Everybody who has or wants to have their own home page
▶ People interested in learning what Java applets are all about

What You Need

Everything you need to create cool Web sites with Java is included on the CD-ROM that comes with this book. It helps if you already have access to the Internet and a Java-compatible Web browser such as HotJava or Netscape Navigator (both are available for downloading). You should know at least a little about HTML to get maximum benefit out of this book. If you want to create your own applets, which we'll show you how to do in the last two chapters, it'll be easier if you know a little programming already. But it isn't necessary to know how to program to use the applets covered in this book.

What You'll Learn

You'll learn many useful techniques for working with Java applets, including how to:

- ▶ add applets to your Web pages without programming
- ▶ mix and match applets with different sounds and images
- ▶ configure applets to meet your own needs
- ▶ create your own applets from scratch

ROADMAP OF THIS BOOK

This book starts off slow and moves to more complex topics. If you're new to Java applets, we suggest you read right through the book, starting at the beginning—where else?

Chapter 1: Introducing Java and Java Applets

This chapter is intended for readers who are a little fuzzy about what Java is and the differences between Java, Java applets, and HotJava. It explains some of the common concepts that you will encounter while reading the rest of this book.

Chapter 2: Java and the Internet

A really important chapter. People who are computer-literate but non-technical should read this chapter to get a good idea of what Java is all about. It describes the language, some of the history, and the unique features that make Java suitable for use on the Internet, particularly on the Web.

Chapter 3: Applets Explained

This chapter introduces the concepts of applets. We'll explain how to add an applet to a home page, how the applet HTML tag works, and how to compile an applet.

Chapter 4: Cool Applets

A "cookbook" chapter that describes a lot of cool applets. All of the applets in this chapter are included on the CD-ROM, and you can use them to design spectacular Java-powered Web pages. We'll give examples of how each applet can be used and how to customize it to fit your needs.

Chapter 5: Java in Depth

This chapter picks up where Chapter 2, Java and the Internet, leaves off. We'll take a closer look at the language and show the basics of programming in it. You should know a little about programming to get the most out of this chapter.

Chapter 6: Building an Applet

This chapter builds on the concepts in Chapter 5. Step-by-step, we'll show you how to build your own Java applets from scratch.

More Information

Aside from reading this book, you can get information on Java applets by browsing the Java/HotJava Web site.

 http://www.javasoft.com/

We've also created a place where you can find more information about this book.

 http://www.javasoft.com/hooked/

ABOUT US

My name is Arthur van Hoff. I've been working on Java and HotJava since 1993. I've helped design the Java Applet API together with Sami. I'm also the author of the Java compiler.

 http://www.javasoft.com/hooked/avh.html

My name is Sami Shaio. I'm the author and implementor of the Java user interface toolkit, and I've designed the applet security mechanisms.

 http://www.javasoft.com/hooked/sami.html

My name is Orca Starbuck. I am a technical writer and a support engineer in the Java project.

 http://www.javasoft.com/hooked/orca.html

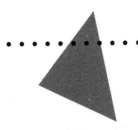

Introducing Java
and Java Applets

With applets written in the Java programming language, Web users can design Web pages that include animation, graphics, games, and other special effects. Most important, Java applets can make Web pages highly interactive. Of course, users need a Java-compliant Web browser like Netscape Navigator or HotJava to view and use Java-powered pages. This chapter explains what Java and Java applets are all about, and why everyone is so excited by them.

WHAT IS JAVA?

If you've picked up this book, chances are you've heard that Java, a new object-oriented programming language developed at Sun Microsystems, is transforming the World-Wide Web. You may be wondering whether this is true or if it's just hype.

Maybe we're a little bit biased because we are part of the programming team that has been developing Java at Sun, but we think it's true. Java allows you to do exciting things with Web pages that weren't possible before.

Greater interactivity is one of the hallmarks of Web pages that use Java. Users can interact with the content of a Java-powered page via the mouse, keyboard, and other user-interface elements such as buttons, slides, and text fields.

Imagine a Web site where you can play a game, such as baseball, that is animated and keeps track of your score. Or a site that has real-time updates to data, such as stock market information. Or a site that offers small applications, such as spreadsheets or calculators, for visitors to use. Or one that shows 3D figures, such as molecules or dinosaurs, that can be rotated with a click of the mouse.

Contrast this level of interactivity with what's currently possible in Web sites that use CGI programming, and you'll be contrasting animation, real-time updates, and applications with e-mail forms and guestbooks that allow users to type comments and send them off. Java pushes the envelope of what's possible on a Web site.

Java can also beef up the multimedia content of a site, offering fluid animation, enhanced graphics, sound, and video without the need for users to hook helper applications into their Web browsers.

What Are Java Applets?

DEFINITION

Java applets are small programs written in Java that are embedded in Web pages to produce special effects.

Small programs written in the Java programming language called Java applets make all this possible. Java applets are embedded right in Web pages. When users access these pages, the applets are downloaded to their computers and executed. Instead of the activity happening on the server side as is the case with CGI programming, it happens on the client side in a Java-compatible Web browser. This means that the applets aren't restricted by network bandwidth or modem access speed when executing. Users see and hear multimedia effects on Web pages in a more effective and timely manner.

Java is an efficient language, so applets that offer user interaction generally operate at the same speed as the other applications on a user's desktop, such as a word processing program.

What Is HotJava?

DEFINITION

HotJava is a Web browser developed by Sun that permits users to view Java-powered Web pages.

To access Web pages with these Java special effects, users need a Java-compatible Web browser. HotJava is one such Web browser, and the first developed. It was created by the Java development team at Sun Microsystems, and it is available for download at the Java Web site. Currently HotJava exists for Windows 95, Windows NT, and Solaris 2.x platforms. But soon HotJava will be available for other systems, including the Mac OS 7.5.

http://www.javasoft.com/

Netscape Navigator also supports Java in version 2.0, which is the latest release. Browsers for Windows 95, Windows NT, and Unix, including Sun Solaris 2.x, are available for download on the Netscape Communications home page.

http://www.netscape.com/

What Are Java-Powered Pages?

Quite simply, Java-powered pages are Web pages that have Java applets embedded in them. They are also the Web pages with the coolest special effects around.

As of the writing of this book, Java is in beta, so the number of sites using Java-powered pages is still building. However, the Cool Java Applets page on the Java/HotJava Web site has plenty of links to Java-powered pages that you should check out. You'll find demos, such as the Financial Portfolio Demo, games such as Hangman and Catch the Jumping Box, special effects such as scrolling images, live feedback image maps, a general-purpose animator, a 3D model viewer, utilities such as a clock, a spreadsheet, and a bar chart, and much more.

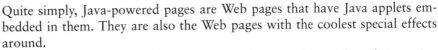

http://www.javasoft.com/applets/applets.html

Remember, you need a Java-compatible Web browser such as HotJava to view and hear these pages and to interact with them; otherwise, all you'll access is static Web pages minus the special effects.

PLUG-N-PLAY APPLETS

Many applets have already been written by the Java development team, by Java enthusiasts, and by us, so it isn't necessary to learn how to program in Java to spice up your Web site with Java applets.

You'll find lots of applets on the CD-ROM that are ready to plug into your Web pages. This includes animation (image loop), nervous text, image maps, scrolling images, bouncing heads, a spreadsheet, tic tac toe, audio effects, clocks, and more (see Chapter 4, "Cool Applets"). We'll show you how to add these applets to your Web pages and how to configure them. You'll be surprised how easy it is.

The CD-ROM also contains Web pages with many of these applets already implemented. You can use these as examples or add them on your Web site.

If you'd like to learn how to build you own applets, we'll cover some of the programming basics of Java that you'll need to know. On the CD-ROM, you'll find the Java Developers Kit (JDK) for Windows 95, Windows NT, and Solaris 2.x, which will prove invaluable when creating your own Java applets. Online documentation for Java APIs is another goodie on the CD-ROM. And, of course, you'll find all the source code from the book.

YOU AND JAVA

Java applets can enrich your Web site and present of wealth of opportunities to engage users through interactivity. We'll show you how to use Java applets to create Web sites that are well worth repeat visits. Just read on!

Java and the Internet

Java is an ideal programming language for Internet applications. In this chapter we'll explain Java's origins, and why it is appropriate for use on the Internet, particularly on the World-Wide Web.

Although Java applets are written in the Java language, it isn't necessary to know how to program in order to use them. If you are just interested in using applets without actually programming in Java, then you can skip this chapter, which introduces the language.

If you want to know more about Java after reading this chapter, see Chapter 5, where we describe the Java programming language in more detail. You can also read the Java language definition. It's available on the Java/HotJava Web site.

 http://www.javasoft.com/hooked/language-ref.html

Java History

The history of a programming language can tell you quite a bit about the language itself. During the design phase, it's important to use the language in real projects. If you don't, the language won't be as useful when it's released, and it won't be much fun to program.

The Java language was used in several projects while it was being designed. Originally Java was intended for use in programming consumer devices. However, it turned out to be a great language for programming for the World-Wide Web.

Origins of Java

The Java programming language was designed and implemented by a small team of people headed by James Gosling at Sun Microsystems in Mountain View, California. In addition to his work on Java, James Gosling is the author of Unix emacs and the NeWS window system.

http://www.javasoft.com/people/jag/index.html

The original Java team worked on designing software for consumer electronics.They quickly found that existing programming languages such as C and C++ were not adequate.

Programs written in C and C++ have to be compiled for a particular computer chip. When a new chip comes out, most software has to be recompiled to make full use of new features on the chips. Once compiled, C and C++ programs are not easily adapted to use new software libraries. The programs have to be recompiled from scratch when the library changes.

Consumer device software has to work on new chips, though, because manufacturers are constrained by the cost of components. If the price of a computer chip becomes too high, they will replace it immediately with a newer, more cost-effective one. Even small price variations can make a big difference when selling millions of devices.

Another problem with using traditional programming languages for consumer device software is that consumer devices generally have a long lifespan. There are working toasters that are 50 years old. The plug still fits into an electrical socket and slices of bread still fit in the slots. Software typically has a much shorter lifespan, which would make it hard to build a toaster with a computer in it. Whenever new software for toasters was written, it would have to be backwardly compatible, because the software in older toasters would need to be replaced.

Software used in consumer electronics must also be very reliable, much more than most computer software. If a consumer product fails, the manufacturer usually has to replace the whole machine.

In 1990, James Gosling started the design of a new programming language that was meant to be more appropriate for consumer electronics, without the problems of traditional languages such as C and C++. The result is Java, a very fast, small, and reliable language that will work for all kinds of computer chips.

The Green Project

The first project that used Java was the Green project. Its purpose was to experiment with a new kind of user interface to control the environment in a

FIGURE **2.1** Duke holding the *7

home (VCR, TV, lights, telephone, pager, and so on). The people working on the Green project built an experimental hand-held computer, code-named the *7 (pronounced "star seven"). In Figure 2.1 Duke, an animated figure from the *7 project, holds the *7 prototype.

The user interface consisted of a full-color, animated representation of the home, in which appliances could be manipulated by touching the screen. It was, of course, completely written in Java. Eight working prototypes of the *7 were built.

The *7 user interface used animated figures on screen to control the appliances. The Java development team still uses some of the artwork from the *7 project. Duke, which is now the Java mascot, was an animated figure in this project (see Figure 2.2).

The follow-on project to the *7 was a video-on-demand (VOD) demo. This project demonstrated that the *7's cartoon-world user interface could be used for interactive television as well as controlling consumer devices.

FIGURE **2.2** Duke

The *7 and the VOD projects resulted in experimental software, but they were not turned into real products. Both projects were entirely implemented in Java and helped to mature the Java language.

WebRunner and HotJava

Around the time Arthur and Sami joined the Java project in 1993, the World-Wide Web was moving from a text-based interface to a more graphical one and generating a lot of interest. It occurred to the Java development team that a platform-neutral language such as Java would be ideal for programming Web applications, because a Java program would run on the many types of computers hooked into the Internet, from PCs to Macs to Unix. The result was a Web browser called WebRunner that was entirely written in Java. Later this browser was renamed HotJava for trademark reasons. HotJava was the first Web browser to support Java applets (see Figure 2.3). You can read more about applets in Chapter 3.

HotJava was an important step for the Java language. It not only matured the language, it also showed off Java to the world. When other programmers saw what the Java development team was doing with HotJava, many wanted to use this new technology in their software, too.

The official announcement of the Java technology was made in May 1995 at the SunWorld conference in San Francisco. At that conference Marc Andreessen,

FIGURE **2.3**   Applet running inside the HotJava browser

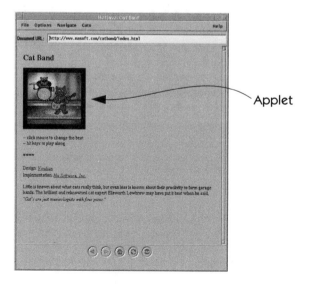

FIGURE 2.4   The Java Development Team

a founder of and the vice president of technology at Netscape Communications, announced that Netscape Navigator would support Java applets. Netscape Navigator 2.0, which shipped at the end of 1995, supports Java and has escalated the already strong interest in Java technology. The Java development team (see Figure 2.4), located in Palo Alto, CA, continues to refine and develop the language and HotJava browser to meet this interest.[1]

 http://www.javasoft.com/hooked/people.html

Why Is It Called Java?

The Java language was originally called Oak by James Gosling. His inspiration for this name was a large oak tree outside of his office window at Sun Microsystems.

Later, the Java development team discovered that Oak was the name of a programming language that predated Sun's language, so another name had to be chosen. It is surprisingly difficult to find a good name for a programming

---

[1] Chuck McManis, Chris Warth, Herb Jellinek, Tim Lindholm, Arthur van Hoff, Michelle Huff, Jonathan Payne, Frank Yellin, Patrick Chan, Erik Gilbert, Eugene Kuerner, Mark Scott Johnson, Richard Tuck, Lisa Friendly, Sami Shaio, Bob Weisblat, James Gosling, Kim Polese, Kathy Walrath.

language, as the team discovered after many hours of brainstorming. Finally, inspiration struck one day during a trip to the local coffee shop.[2]

THE JAVA PROGRAMMING LANGUAGE

Java is a high-level programming language, similar to C, C++, Pascal, and Modula-3.We won't actually teach you how to program in Java in this chapter, but we will show you the basic features of the language. Java is simple, object-oriented, statically typed, compiled, architecture neutral, multi-threaded, garbage collected, robust, secure, and extensible, and well understood. And Java is fun!

Java Is Simple

Java is very similar to C++, but it's much simpler. All the features of high-level programming languages that are not absolutely necessary were left out. For example, Java has no operator overloading, header files, pre-processor, pointer arithmetic, structures, unions, multi-dimensional arrays, templates, or implicit type conversion. Listing 2.1 shows a simple Java program.

LISTING 2.1   A simple Java program

```
1:  public class HelloInternet {
2:     public static void main(String argv[]) {
3:        System.out.println("Hello Internet!");
4:     }
5:  }
```

Java is much easier to learn than C++ because there are fewer concepts. If you know a little C, C++, or Pascal, you'll be hacking in Java in no time.

Java Is Object-Oriented

Java is an object-oriented programming language. With the exception of simple types like numbers and booleans, most things in Java are objects.

http://www.javasoft.com/mem/oo-tutorial.html

---

[2] Java is not an acronym. Despite popular belief, it does not mean "Just Another Vague Acronym."

Java code is organized into classes. Each class defines a set of methods that form the behavior of an object. A class can inherit behaviors from another class. At the root of the class hierarchy is always class Object.

For example, you might define a class Truck, which inherits behaviors from class Car, which in turn inherits from class Vehicle, which inherits from class Object. See Figure 2.5.

Java supports a single-inheritance class hierarchy. This means that each class can only inherit from one other class at a time. Some languages also allow multiple inheritance, but this can be confusing and makes the language unnecessarily complicated. It is hard to imagine, for example, what an object would do that inherits behaviors from two totally different classes, say a Bike and a House.

Not everything in Java is an object. In an effort to make the Java system simpler and more efficient, simple types such as numbers and booleans are not objects. However, Java does provide wrapper objects for all simple types, so that these types can be implemented as classes.

Java also supports interfaces, which are abstract classes. This allows programmers to define methods for interfaces without immediately worrying how the methods will be implemented. A class can implement multiple interfaces. This has many of the advantages as true multiple inheritance, without a lot of the problems. An object can also implement any number of interfaces. The Java interfaces are very similar to IDL[3] interfaces. It is easy to build an

FIGURE **2.5**   Simple Class Hierarchy

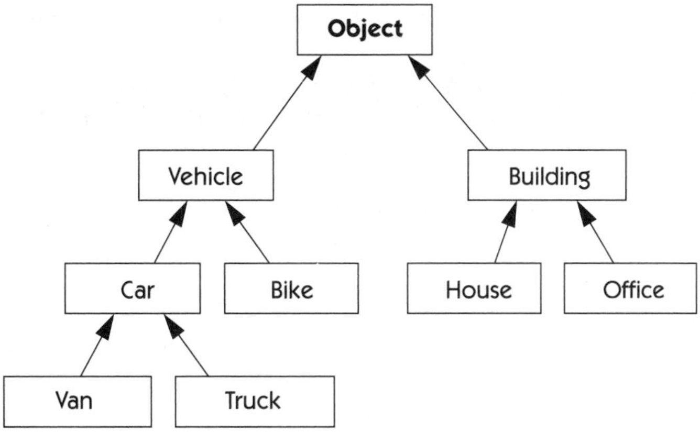

---

[3] Interface Definition Language

IDL-to-Java compiler, which means that Java can be used in the CORBA[4] object system to build distributed object systems. This compatibility is important because both IDL interfaces and the CORBA object system are used in many computer systems.

     `http://www.acl.lanl.gov/sunrise/DistComp/Objects/corba.html`

Java Is Statically Typed

In a Java program, the type of the objects (numbers, characters, arrays, etc.) that are used must be defined. This helps programmers to find potential problems much sooner because type errors can be detected when a program is compiled.

However, all objects in the Java system also have a dynamic type. It is always possible to ask an object for its dynamic type, so a programmer can write programs that do different things for objects of different types.

Most of Java's type checking is done at compile time, which means that the interpreter has to do less work when the program is executed. However, some runtime checks are still required, such as array bounds checking and null pointer checking.

Java Is Compiled

When running a Java program, it's first compiled to *byte-codes*. Byte-codes are very similar to machine instructions, so Java programs can be very efficient. However, byte-codes are not specific to a particular machine, so Java programs can be executed on lots of different computers without recompiling the programs.

Java source programs are compiled to *class files*, which contain the byte-code representation of the program. In a Java class file, all references to methods and instance variables are made by name and are resolved when the code is first executed. This makes the code more general and less susceptible to changes, but still efficient.

Java Is Architecture Neutral

Because Java programs are compiled to byte-codes, they can run on any platform that supports Java. It isn't necessary to recompile a Java program to run on a new machine.

The Java language is the same on every computer. For example, simple types don't vary: an integer is always 32 bits and a long is always 64 bits. Sur-

---

[4] Common Object Request Broker Architecture

prisingly, this is not true for modern programming languages such as C and C++. Because these languages are so loosely defined, each compiler and development environment is slightly different, which makes porting a nightmare. Porting Java programs is easy, and it isn't necessary to recompile them.

The Java system also provides an extensive library of classes that provides access to the underlying operating system. When these libraries are used, Java programs will work on any platform where Java is supported. A complete set of hyperlinked API documentation for these libraries, listed below, is on the CD-ROM included with this book.

java.lang   General language classes such as Object, String, Number, Exception, Error, etc.

java.util   Useful utility classes such as Hashtable, Vector, Enumeration, Properties, etc.

java.io   Streams-based Input and Output. These classes provide access to the file system.

java.net   Networking classes. These classes provide access to TCP/IP sockets, Internet Addresses, and URLs.

java.awt   The Abstract Window Toolkit. A cross-platform graphical user interface toolkit.

java.applet   Support for applets (embeddable Java programs).

 http://www.javasoft.com/hooked/api/packages.html

Java Is Multi-Threaded

Most modern computer systems such as Unix and Windows 95 support multi-tasking, which means that the computer is able to perform more than one task at the same time. Java has support for multi-tasking built into the language.

A Java program can have more than one *thread* of execution. For example, it could perform some lengthy computation in one thread, while other threads interact with the user. So users do not have to stop working to wait for Java programs to complete lengthy operations.

Programming in a multi-threaded environment is usually difficult because many things can happen at the same time or in an unpredictable order. Java, however, provides easy-to-use features for synchronization that make programming easier.

Java threads are usually mapped onto real operating system threads if the underlying operating system supports this action. Thus applications written in Java are *MP-hot*, which means they will benefit if they are executed on a multi-processor machine.

Java Is Garbage Collected

Programmers who write software in C and C++ have to keep careful track of each chunk of memory used. When a chunk is no longer used, they have to make sure the program frees it so that it can be used again. In large projects this can become difficult, and it is often a source of bugs and memory leaks.

In Java, programmers don't have to worry about memory management. The Java system has a built-in program called the *garbage collector* that scans memory and automatically frees any memory chunk that is no longer in use. It makes Java programs a lot simpler to write, and programmers never have to worry about memory management.

Java Is Robust

Anyone who works on a personal computer knows how frustrating it can be when the computer crashes because of a bug in a program. It's possible to lose a lot of work that way.

Java programs can't cause a computer to crash. The Java system carefully checks each access to memory and makes sure it's legal and won't cause any problems.

But even Java programs can have bugs. If something unexpected happens, the program doesn't crash, but an *exception* is thrown. The program will find these exceptions and deal with them.

Traditional programs can access all of your computer's memory. A program can (unintentionally) change any value in memory, which can cause problems. Java programs can only access those parts of memory that they are allowed to access, so a Java program cannot change a value that it's not supposed to change.

Java Is Small

Because Java was designed to run on small computers, the Java system is relatively small for a programming language. It can run efficiently on personal computers with 4Mb of RAM or more. The Java interpreter takes up only a few hundred kilobytes. The interpreter is responsible for Java's platform independence and portability.

The *7 machine discussed earlier in this chapter had 3Mb of main memory. It ran a small Unix operating system and a Java interpreter, with enough space left over to run fairly media-rich software. Because the Java runtime is small, it is ideal for computers with very little memory such as the *7, as well as TVs, toasters, telephones, and home computers.

Java Is Fast

Java is a lot more efficient than typical scripting languages, but it is about 20 times slower than C. This, however, is acceptable for most applications.

In the near future code generators will be available that will make Java programs nearly as fast as programs written in C or C++.

Java Is Secure

Java programs have no pointers, and byte-code programs like Java are strongly typed, so it is possible to verify a Java program before executing it. A verified Java program is guaranteed not to break any of the Java language constraints and can be safely executed. Java byte-code verification is used by Web browsers to make sure that applets don't contain viruses. You'll find more information on Java security later in this chapter.

    http://www.javasoft.com/hooked/security.html

Java Is Extensible

It is also possible to interface Java programs to existing software libraries written in other languages. Because Java data structures are very similar to C's data structures and types, this is relatively easy. The biggest problem is that most existing libraries are not multi-threaded.

A Java program can declare certain methods to be *native*. These native methods are then mapped to functions defined in software libraries that are dynamically linked into the virtual machine. Although it is possible to dynamically link in any native software library, it is not always allowed. For security reasons this feature is usually disabled for software that is loaded over the network.

We hope that in the future it won't be necessary to link in any software libraries, because they can all be written in Java. This will be practical when Java becomes just as fast as C and C++.

Java Is Well Understood

The cool Java features mentioned in this chapter are not new. Some of these features were invented for other languages such as Lisp, Smalltalk, Pascal, Cedar, Objective-C, Self, and Beta. Java is simply a good mix of existing technologies.

Because of this, Java's underlying technology is well understood, although the language itself is new. The coming years will see many new and exciting advances in Java technology.

Java Is Fun

Last but not least, Java is a lot of fun to program in. Because it is harder to make stupid mistakes with Java, programmers spend a lot less time chasing memory smashes and unexplainable core dumps. It is easier to be productive when programming with Java. We've been using Java for several years, and we love it.

JAVA AND THE INTERNET

The Internet is a gigantic network that connects many thousands of computers together. It is a heterogeneous network, because so many different types of computers are connected. All these computers use the TCP/IP protocol to communicate. That means that a PC can communicate just as easily with a Mac as it can with another PC.

Because there are so many different computer systems connected to each other, they need a language that is not tied to a particular platform to exchange programs. Java is ideal for this purpose (see Figure 2.6).

Java programs are transmitted as byte-codes, which means that they can run on any computer without needing to be compiled. It is possible to download a Java program to any computer on the Internet and execute it without worrying about the system on which the program was developed.

With traditional compiled languages, this would not be possible. These languages require compilation for a particular platform, and the resulting pro-

FIGURE 2.6   The heterogeneous Internet

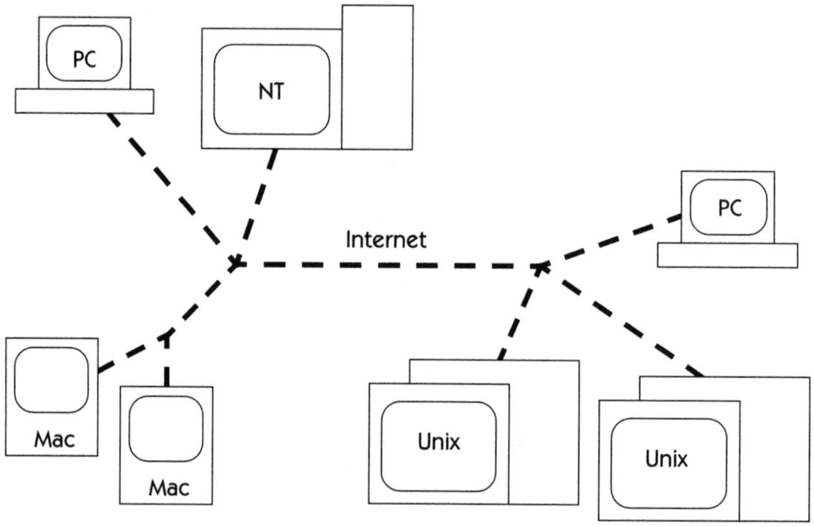

gram cannot be executed on a different system. To use a C program on multiple platforms, a programmer would have to distribute source code and each user would have to compile the program before running it.

Java Applets

Because Java is a good language for Internet programming, the Java team decided to use it to implement a World-Wide Web browser with interactive content. This became HotJava.

HotJava is able to download Java applets as part of a Web page. Each applet is executed and displayed inside the browser. Java is a great language for this purpose because Java programs can run on any computer without recompiling, and Java is secure.

HotJava was the first browser to support downloading and executing Java applets, but it's not the only one. Netscape Navigator 2.0 also supports Java applets.

Security

Because Java applets are downloaded to your computer and executed automatically when you view Java-powered pages, you might think that there is a risk of a virus infecting your machine. This is not the case. No Java applet is able to steal information or damage your computer in any way.

The reason that Java applets are secure is that Java programs are compiled into byte-code instructions, which can be verified. Byte-code instructions are very similar to other instruction sets used by computers, but they are not specific to a particular computer system and they can be checked for potential security violations. This is possible because the Java byte-codes contain additional type information that is used to verify that the program is legal. See Figure 2.7.

Most programs for the PC call functions by address. Because the address is simply a number and that number can be constructed any way the program likes, the program can use any number to execute a function. This makes it impossible to tell which functions will be used when the program is actually invoked.

Java uses a totally different approach. Methods and variables are always accessed by name. This makes it easy to determine what methods and functions are actually used. This process is called *verification*. It is needed to ensure that the byte-codes haven't been tampered with and that they obey the Java language constraints.

Once the Java applet has been verified, it is executed in a restricted environment. Applets cannot execute certain dangerous functions in this environment

FIGURE 2.7   The Java byte-code verification process

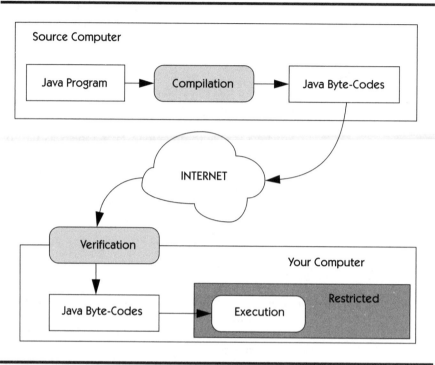

unless they are allowed to do so. Because of the verification process, the applet is not able to break out of this restricted environment.

Once the Java byte-codes have been verified, the Java interpreter can turn the function names into addresses, just like traditional programs. This means that Java programs can be efficient and secure at the same time.

THE FUTURE OF JAVA

Java has to potential to revolutionize the Web by changing the way software is delivered on the Internet. It is an entirely new technology that could be used in ways we haven't yet started to explore. Java as a general programming language will fill an important role in the next generation of Internet software.

Currently, Java applets are embedded in Web pages, but this may change. Perhaps the browser itself will be applets that are downloaded to your computer as you need them. This would mean that you would always be running the latest version of a browser. If you want a browser for a format other than HTML, just visit a page on the Web, and the appropriate browser/editor is downloaded from the net.

Futurists exposed to Java speculate that Java may even replace the way we use applications. It could become possible to access an application, such as a word processing program or a spreadsheet, while we're online, from the application company whenever we needed to use the program. We'd be charged only for the time that we used the application, and we'd be assured of getting the latest version of software. Contrast this to the way we use applications today: it's necessary to buy a separate application for each type of task we wish to accomplish, and pay again to upgrade when new versions are released.

If the Internet continues to grow at its current rate, a lot of people who are connected to the Internet will be new computer users. The Internet will become a place for consumers, rather then programmers. Java will play an important role in this world, because it is flexible and it hides a lot of the nitty-gritty details that Internet users now have to deal with.

We believe that the Internet will be a more interesting place to be, thanks to Java.

3

Applets Explained

In this chapter, we explain how Java applets work and how you add them to a Web page. You should finish this chapter before reading Chapter 4, "Cool Applets." You'll learn everything you need to know to add an applet from the CD-ROM to your home page.

JAVA APPLETS

Java applets are treated by your Java-compatible browser just like other media objects in a Web page, such as image, audio, and video files. The applet's byte-code files (also called class files) are loaded into the browser, where they are verified and executed (see Figure 3.1).

Like images, applets are displayed as part of the page. The page's text flows around the space taken up by the applet. Once the applet is loaded, it can present special effects, such as animation, graphics, sound, real-time data up-dates, applications, and more, and interact with the user through the mouse, keyboard, and user interface elements like buttons, slides, and text fields.

Java-Compatible Browsers

Any browser carrying the "Java Compatible" logo is able to run Java applets. Currently, you can choose between the beta version of Sun Microsystem's HotJava browser (see Figure 3.2) or Netscape Navigator version 2.0 (there are more to follow).

Java-compatible browsers provide a set of standard libraries that every Java applet can use. As long as the applet uses only these libraries, it will work in any Java-compatible browser. So your applets will run just as well in HotJava

JAVA™ COMPATIBLE

FIGURE 3.1   Applet running inside Netscape Navigator

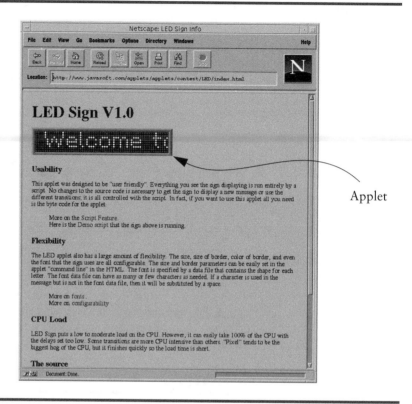

Applet

on Solaris 2.3 as they do in Netscape Navigator on Windows 95, even if you developed them on a different computer. This is possible because of Java's architecture neutral byte-codes (see "Java Is Architecture Neutral" on page 12 in Chapter 2, "Java and the Internet").

Web pages that contain Java applets sometimes have the "Java Powered" logo to indicate that the page is best displayed in a Java-compatible browser. You can still view the page with another browser, but you'll most likely not see the applets.

The CD-ROM contains a useful tool called the Appletviewer. It'll let you view Java applets, without having to use a Java-compatible browser. You can use it to view the applets on the CD-ROM, even if you are not connected to the Internet. We'll cover this in more detail in "The Appletviewer" on page 30 later in this chapter.

Applet Functionality

Applets have access to a wide range of functionality via a set of libraries that let them perform a variety of interesting operations. These libraries are part

FIGURE 3.2 The HotJava browser

of the Java Applet API,[1] and the API is supported by all Java-compatible browsers.

A networking library for low-level TCP/IP[2] socket I/O[3], as well as high-level URL operations, is used by applets to download resources or to communicate with other computers on the Internet. There are some security restrictions with respect to the hosts that can be accessed by an applet, but more about that later in this chapter.

An elaborate set of graphics routines are used by applets to draw to the screen. In addition to the normal operations to draw lines, circles, text, and so on, applets also have access to a powerful set of image-handling routines, so they can download large images.

---

[1] Application Programming Interface

[2] Transmission Control Protocol/Internet Protocol—a set of communication protocols that are the basis of the Internet

[3] Input/Output

One of the most important parts of the Java Applet API is the Abstract Window Toolkit (also called the AWT). It lets applets create user-interface components such as windows, buttons, sliders, and scrollbars. The AWT uses your computer's native GUI[4] widgets, so applets will have the same look as other applications.

Applets also have access to a library for playing audio files, so you can add audio effects to a Web page. It is likely that the audio library will be further improved, and applets will be able to do even more elaborate audio effects.

Applet Examples

Applets are rapidly becoming popular. You can find several categories of applets on the net:

- ▶ Animation
- ▶ Games
- ▶ Collaboration
- ▶ Internet Shopping
- ▶ Productivity Applications
- ▶ Client/Server Access

Here are some good starting points for finding new applets.

 http://www.javasoft.com/applets/AppletSites.html

 http://www.netscape.com/

 http://www.dimensionx.com/

How Applets Work

Applets are added to Web pages with the <applet> tag. This tag is used to describe the applet, its width and height, and its parameters. When your Java-compatible browser encounters an <applet> tag, it downloads the code for the applet and executes the applet.

LISTING 3.1 A home page with an applet

```
1:  <title>Arthur's Home Page</title>
2:  <h1>Welcome to my home page!</h1>
3:  As you can see, this page still needs a lot of work. Please come back soon.
```

---

[4] Graphical User Interface

```
4:  <p>
5:  <applet code=JackhammerDuke.class width=300 height=80>
6:  </applet>
7:  <address>avh@eng.sun.com</address>
```

Listing 3.1 shows the source for an early version of Arthur's home page. You'll find an applet referenced on lines 6 and 7. As you can see in Figure 3.3, the applet appears below the first paragraph of text when the page is viewed with a browser.

Note that the applet, just like an image file, needs some time to load to your computer. So it may take a few seconds, depending on the speed of your link to the Internet, before the applet actually appears on your screen.

Once the applet is loaded, it will run as quickly as any other application on your computer. The applet can download other resources like images, audio files, or more Java code while running. It can also interact with you. Not all applets are interactive, though; some applets simply display animation or graphics.

Applet Parameters

Applets have parameters that you can specify in an HTML file. You can customize an applet by using these parameters and never have to program a line of Java code.

FIGURE 3.3   An early version of Arthur's home page

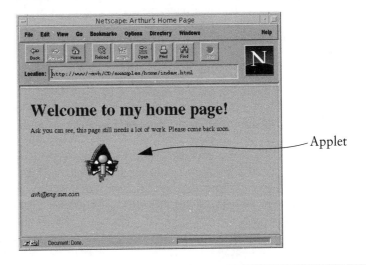

A well-written Java applet will have a comprehensive set of parameters that'll let you change most of its important aspects. An example is the ImageLoop applet (see "Animator" in Chapter 4, "Cool Applets"), which animates an image (see Listing 3.2). ImageLoop has parameters that determine the image that is loaded (line 3), the size of the image (line 1), the number of frames (line 2), and the speed at which the animation is run (line 4). By changing these parameters, you can use it to display many different animations.

LISTING 3.2   The ImageLoop applet

```
1:   <applet code=ImageLoopItem width=80 height=90>
2:   <param name=nimgs value=10>
3:   <param name=img value=duke>
4:   <param name=pause value=1000>
5:   </applet>
```

Chapter 4, "Cool Applets," describes many applets with their parameters. All of these applets are included on the CD-ROM. You can use them as is, or configure their parameters to fit your needs. You don't need to program in Java to use or configure them.

We'll explain more about specifying applet parameters in "Applet Tag" on page 35 in this chapter.

ADDING AN APPLET TO YOUR HOME PAGE

In this section, we'll briefly explain what you need to do to add an applet to your home page. As an example, we will use the ImageLoop applet from the CD-ROM.

Creating Your Home Page

If you don't have a home page or if you are not connected to the Web, you can still try out your first applet. Simply make a directory on your hard disk (call it home page or whatever you like), and create a file called index.html (or index.htm, if your platform is Windows 3.1 or DOS) in that directory.

You can use any text editor, word-processing program, or HTML editor that you are familiar with to create and edit your home page—as long as it can work with ASCII files. For instance in Windows 95, you can use Word-Pad, Word for Windows, or Internet Assistant. If you want to learn more about writing HTML, check out this URL:

http://www.ncsa.uiuc.edu/General/Internet/WWW/HTMLPrimer.html

Listing 3.3 shows an example of a very simple home page.

LISTING 3.3 Source code for a simple home page

```
1:  <title>My Home Page</title>
2:  <h1>Welcome</h1>
3:  Hello and welcome to my home page.
```

If you want your home page to be accessible by other Internet users, you'll have to install an http server on your computer and get an Internet connection, or you'll have to post your pages on a site operated by an Internet services provider. To find tutorials on the Web that tell you how to do this, Yahoo is a good place to start.

  http://www.yahoo.com

Copying the Applet

To add an applet to your Web pages, you first have to copy it into the same directory as your home page. As an example, we'll copy the contents of the ImageLoop applet directory from the CD-ROM into the home-page directory you created that contains index.html. Figure 3.4 shows what the directory should look like after you've copied the applet into it.

The directory now contains your home page (index.html), the source code to the ImageLoop applet (ImageLoopItem.java), the Java class files for the applet

FIGURE 3.4 Home-page directory structure

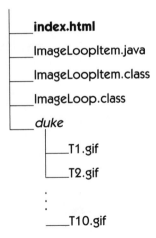

(ImageLoopItem.class, ImageLoop.class), and a directory containing the 10 frames of animation (duke).

Editing Your Home Page

Now that you've copied the applet into the right place, you can edit your home page and add the <applet> tag. This will embed the applet in the page.

LISTING 3.4   A simple home page with an applet

```
1:  <title>My Home Page</title>
2:  <h1>Welcome</h1>
3:  Hello, welcome to my home page.
4:  <p>
5:  <applet code=ImageLoopItem width=80 height=90>
6:  <param name=nimgs value=10>
7:  <param name=img value=duke>
8:  <param name=pause value=1000>
9:  </applet>
```

Note the <p> tag on line 4 of Listing 3.4. It is needed to make sure that the applet appears on a new line. Without it, the applet would appear in the text right after the word "page."

Now that you've added the <applet> tag to your home page, you're ready to load the page in a Java-compatible browser (see Figure 3.5).

FIGURE 3.5   Using a browser to view the Imageloop applet

FIGURE 3.6   Using the Appletviewer to view the Imageloop applet

You can also view the applet in your home page with the Appletviewer. We'll explain in more detail how to use the Appletviewer in the next section, but for now at the prompt (or within the Run dialog box in Windows 95 and Windows NT) try typing:[5]

```
appletviewer index.html
```

This should start the Appletviewer, and you'll see the applet that you've added to your home page in its own window (see Figure 3.6).

HTML Editors

HotJava contains a WYSIWYG[6] HTML editor that will let you edit your HTML files. (See Figure 3.7.) With it, you can also add applets to Web pages by using the copy and paste features or by entering the applet parameters in a dialog box.

At the time this book was written, it was unclear when HotJava with the HTML editor would be available to the public. Check out the Java/HotJava home page for the latest information:

   http://www.javasoft.com/

JAVA APPLET TOOLS

We've included Sun Microsystems' Java Developers Kit (JDK) for Solaris 2.x, Windows 95, and Windows NT on the CD-ROM. The JDK contains a number of essential tools that you need to develop applets.

---

[5] You may have to type in the full path name for the appletviewer application on your CD-ROM.

[6] What You See Is What You Get

FIGURE 3.7   HTML editing with HotJava

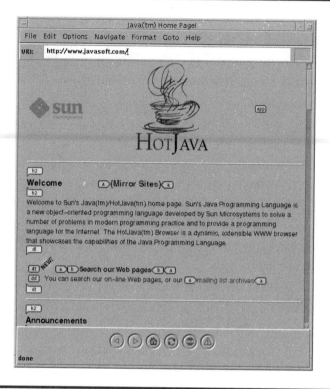

If you don't have access to a Java-compatible browser, you can use the Appletviewer in the JDK to run applets. You may want to try the Appletviewer anyway, because it's a useful tool for testing applets. All the applets in this book are included on the CD-ROM, so you don't need an Internet connection to get started. We've even provided the source code.

The JDK on the CD-ROM contains:

▶ javac—Java compiler
▶ java—Java interpreter
▶ jdb—Java debugger
▶ appletviewer—Java applet viewer
▶ Applet API documentation
▶ Java Programming Guide

The Appletviewer

The Appletviewer takes one or more files as arguments. It loads the Web pages in these files and displays the applets found in the pages (see Figure 3.8).

FIGURE 3.8   Running an applet in the Appletviewer

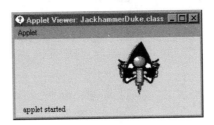

DEFINITION

The **Appletviewer** is a tool for viewing applets. It is part of the JDK and is included on the CD-ROM.

You can also invoke the Appletviewer and pass an URL to it as an argument, so you can view applets on other Web sites. You need Internet access to do this, and you'll also need to configure the Appletviewer (see "Configuring the Appletviewer" on page 32). For instance, you can view the applets on the Java/HotJava home page by typing the following command at the prompt or the Run dialog box:

```
appletviewer http://www.javasoft.com/
```

When you pass more than one file or URL to the Appletviewer, or if the Web page contains more than one applet, the Appletviewer will open multiple windows, one for each applet.

Appendix F, "Appletviewer," is the manual page for the Appletviewer, and it contains more information on this tool.

The Appletviewer Menu

Each Appletviewer window has an Applet menu that lets you perform the following operations:

Restart   This stops the applet and starts it again. However, it may not have much effect on applets that don't observe the start and stop methods.

Reload   You can use this operation to avoid restarting the Appletviewer when you've changed an applet's code. It'll reload the applet from scratch, and it's particularly useful if the applet has been recompiled.

Clone   This operation creates another copy of the applet. The new applet is shown in a new window, and it's started from scratch.

Tag   A window pops up that displays the HTML tag for this applet. You can copy and paste the applet tag into an HTML document.

Info	This operation shows additional information about the applet's parameters in a pop-up window. Not all applets have additional information, however.
Properties	You can set networking and security options for the Appletviewer with this operation. We'll explain it in more detail in the next section.
Close	This operation closes the current Appletviewer window. The Appletviewer program will terminate when you've closed all Appletviewer windows.

Configuring the Appletviewer

To configure the Appletviewer's properties, you have to select Properties from the Applet menu. This will show a dialog box, in which you can enter properties that are needed to run the Appletviewer successfully over the Internet (see Figure 3.9).

The Appletviewer's properties window lets you edit the following properties:

HTTP proxy server	The name of your HTTP proxy server. Ask your system administrator or your Internet services provider what you should enter here.
HTTP proxy port	The port number on your HTTP proxy server. The proxy port number is usually 80.

FIGURE 3.9   Configuring the Appletviewer

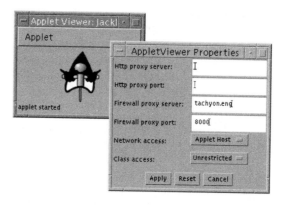

Firewall proxy server
The name of your firewall proxy server. This is needed if you are using the Appletviewer from inside a company that has a firewall. Check with your system administrator what you should enter.

Firewall proxy port
The port number of your firewall proxy server. This port number is usually set to 80.

Network access
This pull-down menu controls what parts of the network applets are able to access. The options are: None, Applet Host, and Unrestricted. See "Applet Security Modes" below for detailed information on what each mode means.

Class access
This pull-down menu controls which classes applets can access. The choices are: Unrestricted and Restricted. Although the default setting is unrestricted, you can set it to restricted if you want to make sure that your applets don't access classes that are not available in all Java-compatible browsers.

To access applets over the Internet with the Appletviewer, you have to set the HTTP proxy server and HTTP proxy port properties. Also, you need to make sure that the security mode is set to Applet Host.

Applet Security Modes

The HotJava browser supports several security modes.[7] You can usually set the security mode in the properties or preferences dialog box.

Here is a quick overview:

None
Applets will not be allowed to access the network. You should choose this mode only if you are extremely worried about security violations. Some applets may not work in this mode.

Applet Host
In this mode, applets are allowed to access data only on their host, which means that applets from other systems will not be able to access information on your computers. This is the default security mode, and most applets will work in this mode. Figure 3.10 shows what an applet can access in this mode.

Firewall
This mode differentiates between applets that are inside your company's firewall and ones that are outside. Applets outside of the firewall can only access resources that are also outside of the

DEFINITION

A **firewall** restricts external access to large company networks.

_____

[7] The Netscape Navigator beta release only supports Applet Host mode.

FIGURE 3.10   Applet host security mode

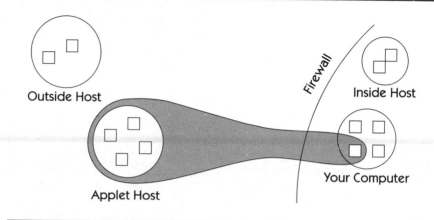

firewall. Figure 3.11 shows what an applet outside of the firewall can access. To use this mode, the firewall must be set up correctly.

Unrestricted   Most applets can make connections to any host on the Internet in this mode. However, this mode is potentially dangerous if you are inside a company. Applets will be able to access and transmit any information that is available over the Internet. You should only select this mode if you are not concerned about security.

FIGURE 3.11   Firewall security mode

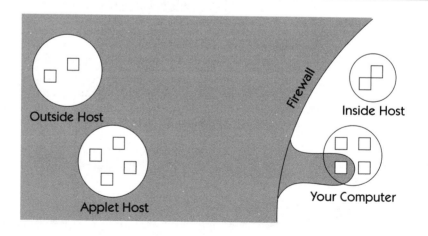

APPLETS BASICS

Applet Tag

The `<applet>` tag[8] is an HTML command just like the tag for changing the text style to bold `<b>`...`</b>`.

The `<applet>` tag is not a standard HTML tag, and it's supported only by browsers that understand applets. Other browsers will simply ignore this tag when they see it.

LISTING 3.5 Applet tag description

```
1:  <applet standard-attributes>
2:  applet-parameters
3:  alternate-content
4:  </applet>
```

Listing 3.5 show the structure of the applet tag. Standard attributes are included at the beginning of applet tag (line 1). Some of these attributes are required, whereas some are optional. Applet parameters are non-standard attributes that apply only to the applet in question (line 2).

Alternate content (line 3) can contain HTML commands that will get executed only if the browser viewing the page doesn't understand applets. Such a browser will ignore the other applet components and show only the alternate content.

LISTING 3.6 Applet tag example

```
1:  <applet code="HelloWorld.class" width=100 height=30>
2:  <param name=text value="Hello World!">
3:  Get a <b>Java-</b>powered browser!
4:  </applet>
```

Line 1 of Listing 3.6 shows the applet start tag. It is used to specify the applet's required attributes: `code`, `width`, `height`. Line 2 describes an applet parameter named `text`, which contains a string, `"Hello World!"` Line 3 contains the alternate content, which is only displayed by browsers that don't support Java applets. The last line contains the applet end tag, which every applet must have.

---

[8] See Appendix G, "Applet Tag Definition," for the formal specification of the `<applet>` tag.

Attributes are usually specified as *name=value*. The value can be anything, but if it contains characters other than letters and digits, you should put quotes around it, as we did in Listing 3.6.

Required Applet Attributes

Let's look at the required applet attributes first, which all applets *must* have. The required attributes are:

code	The name of the file that contains the main class of the applet. This is usually a file name ending in ".class." The file name is relative to the optional attribute codebase, but it isn't allowed to be an absolute URL.
width	Specifies the initial width of the applet in pixels.
height	Specifies the initial height of the applet in pixels.

Optional Applet Attributes

These attributes are optional. You can use them to specify where the applet is loaded from and how it is positioned on the page.

codebase	The base URL of the applet. The applet's code is located relative to this URL. If this attribute isn't specified, then it defaults to the URL of the document in which the applet is specified.
alt	Alternate text that can be displayed by text-only browsers.
name	The symbolic name of the applet. This name can be used by applets on the same page to locate this applet.
align	The alignment of the applet. This affects where the applet is placed on the page. It can be one of the following alignments: left, right, top, texttop, middle, absmiddle, baseline, bottom, absbottom. See "Positioning an Applet" later in this chapter for more information.
vspace	The vertical space around the applet. This attribute is used only when the align attribute is set to left or right.
hspace	The horizontal space around the applet. This attribute is used only when the align attribute is set to left or right.

Additional Applet Parameters

Applets often use additional applet-specific parameters, as well as the predefined applet attributes. They are specified in a separate <param> tag instead of inside the applet start tag.

The <param> tag itself has two attributes, name and value, that let you specify a name and a value. For example:

LISTING 3.7 Applet parameters

```
1:  <applet class=GotoButton.class width=200 height=30>
2:  <param name=label value=Home>
3:  <param name=dest value="http://www.javasoft.com/">
4:  </applet>
```

On line 2 of Listing 3.7, a parameter called label is defined to have the value Home. On line 3, a parameter called dest is used to point at the Java/Hot-Java home page.

Each applet recognizes a different set of applet parameters, in addition to the standard applet attributes. Chapter 4, "Cool Applets," describes in detail the applet-specific parameters for each applet.

Alternate Applet Content

You can include any kind of HTML content (text and tags) between the last applet parameter and the end tag. This content is not displayed by Java-compatible browsers, but it is displayed by browsers that ignore the <applet> tag. For example, the text on line 3 in Listing 3.6 is displayed only by non-Java-compatible browsers.

You can also use the alt attribute of the <applet> tag to specify alternative text that can be displayed instead of the applet. This text is displayed in some text-only browsers or it is displayed while the applet is being loaded.

Positioning an Applet

You can position an applet just like you position images in a Web page. The align attribute defines how an applet can be positioned with respect to the surrounding text. The effect of this attribute on the applet is the same as the align attribute of the <img> tag.

The most interesting values for the align attribute are left and right. With these values, the text flows around the applet. The amount of white space around the applet is defined by the vspace and hspace attributes. Note that you can also use tables to arrange the applets on your Web page.

Applet Resources

An applet can consist of a number of different files. You will need to understand where to place these files to add applets to your Web pages successfully.

▶ Java class files (.class)—These files contain the Java byte-codes for the applet. They are generated by the Java compiler (see "Java Is Compiled" on page 12 in Chapter 2, "Java and the Internet").

▶ Java source files (.java)—You don't need the applet's source files in order to use the applet. Some applets (such as the ones on the CD-ROM) contain source files for reference.

▶ Image files (.gif,.jpeg)—These files contain images that are loaded by the applet once it's running.

▶ Audio files (.au)—These are the audio files used by the applet, and they are loaded once the applet is running.

▶ Data files—These files are applet-specific and contain data that the applet needs. They can be in any format that the applet likes, so you'll need to check out the documentation for the applet.

▶ HTML files—Most applets provide some examples of how they can be used in the form of HTML files. You can use the Appletviewer on these files to try the applets out.

Figure 3.12 shows the directory structure of the UnderConstruction applet. This applet is located in a subdirectory of the directory in which the Web page (index.html) is located.

Because this applet is not located in the document directory (index.html), you need to set the codebase attribute to the applet's location (see Listing 3.8).

The codebase attribute can be the name of a directory relative to the location of the document (Web page) or it can be a URL. In the case of an URL, the applet does not have to be located near your document at all. It can be anywhere on the Internet.

LISTING **3.8**   **Using the codebase attribute**

```
1:  <applet codebase=UnderConstruction
2:        code=JackHammerDuke.class
3:        width=300 height=100>
4:  </applet>
```

FIGURE **3.12**   The directory structure of a typical applet

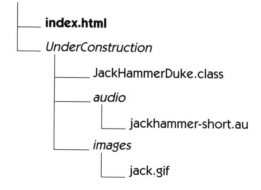

Listing 3.8 shows an example of how you can include an applet that is not located in the same directory as your Web page. The codebase attribute specifies that the applet is actually located in a subdirectory called UnderConstruction. If you set the codebase attribute to http://www.javasoft.com/hooked/UnderConstruction, the applet is loaded from that location.

Note that the resources specified in the applet parameters are always considered to be relative to the document or Web page, unless you specify an absolute URL.

Compiling an Applet

In case you are interested in modifying applets from the CD-ROM, or if you want to write an applet from scratch, you will need to use the Java compiler. To run the compiler, simply change directories until you're in the directory containing the applet. Then use the javac command to compile Java source files in the directory.

If there are errors in the program, they will be printed on the standard output. The error messages contain a file name and line number. Please refer to the Java language manual for more information.

 http://www.javasoft.com/hooked/language-ref.html

Performance Tuning

Applets consist of many small files that are each downloaded individually. This can be slow because it usually takes a fairly long time to establish connections on the Internet. This is unrelated to the speed of the connection to the Internet that you're using.

In the near future, we hope that this problem will be resolved by the acceptance of a new http standard like http-ng. In the meantime, some browsers may be using the keep-alive feature supported by some http servers. Both these solutions avoid the need of making multiple connections in order to download an applet.

 http://www.w3.org/hypertext/WWW/Protocols/HTTP-NG/http-ng-status.html

Another performance problem can be your connection to the Internet. Applet code is usually relatively small, so it should download more quickly than most images. However, most applets use images and audio, which again will mean slow downloading.

A good way to improve the overall performance of your browser is to use a caching http proxy server. It will save files that you have downloaded to disk, so if you reference them again, you access them from your hard drive instead of the Internet. This won't speed up the downloading of applets the first time, but it makes the second time much faster!

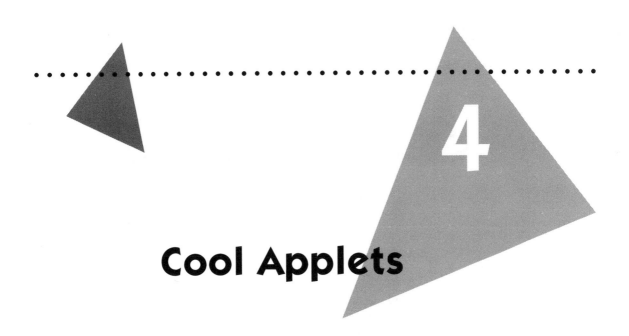

Cool Applets

This chapter describes the various applets that are included with this book and shows you how to use each one. Most of them can be customized to better suit your needs.

The majority of the applets covered here are simple to plug into your Web pages and to configure. We tried to select ones that are also useful and interesting. All the applets in this chapter are on the CD-ROM, ready to use in your own Web site.

After this book is published, many more applets will be written. Check out the following URL for an up-to-date list of applets:

   http://www.javasoft.com/applets/

OVERVIEW

We've included a wide variety of applets in this book: text effects, interactive graphics, games and educational applications, and many more. Most of the applets we selected for this book are simple ones that can be used easily in your Web pages. Some are more complex.

To get you started, this chapter is in essence a catalog of all the applets included on the CD-ROM. In this "catalog," you'll find a description of each applet, parameters specific to it, examples of the applet tags, formats that the applet may use, and comments and hints from us. We've also included pictures of Web pages that use these applets, so you can get a feel for what they may look like or do. The applets are listed in alphabetical order for easy reference. Appendix A, "Applet Guide" also contains a complete list of the applets.

Instant Applets

We've included some very simple applets that you can drop into a Web page to spice it up. For these applets, you don't even need to add an image or sound file.

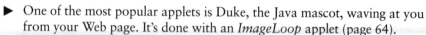

- ▶ One of the most popular applets is Duke, the Java mascot, waving at you from your Web page. It's done with an *ImageLoop* applet (page 64).
- ▶ With the *Tumbling Duke* applet (page 84), Duke dances back and forth across your page.
- ▶ Duke gets out his jackhammer for the *Under Construction* applet (page 85).
- ▶ The animated *What's New!* applet (page 87) is a good way to make new information really stand out on a page.
- ▶ The *Clock* applet (page 58) displays an analog clock.

Animation and Audio

These are applets that play sounds or display animated images. Use them with your own images and sounds for appealing effects.

- ▶ The *AudioItem* applet (page 49) plays a sound, background music, or any other audio clip.
- ▶ The *ImageLoop* applet (page 64) rapidly displays a sequence of images to create animation.
- ▶ The *Animator* applet (page 47) is like ImageLoop, but it also lets you specify many more features, such as background audio, and audio for individual frames.
- ▶ The *Scrolling Images* applet (page 79) displays a panoramic view or a collection of images scrolling across the page.

Interactive Graphics

Here's a collection of applets that display images or draw graphics and allow you to manipulate or click on the images for various effects. Interactive applets such as these are not only a flashy addition to your Web pages, they can also be very useful.

- ▶ The *ImageMap* applet (page 65) allows you to create image maps with live feedback as you move your mouse across the image. It is one of the most useful general-purpose applets.
- ▶ The *Link Button* applet (page 72) is a more specialized sort of image map. It creates a simple button that links to another URL.

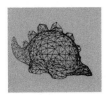

▶ The *Zine* applet (page 90) creates a different sort of active image. Boxed captions pop up when you move the mouse across the image.

▶ The *Wire Frame Viewer* applet (page 88) draws a wire-frame image based on your specifications that can be rotated with the mouse. We've used it to draw a dinosaur.

Text Tricks

Applets that feature dazzling text effects can be used to emphasize a headline or just to amuse visitors to your site. Here are a selection of cool text tricks.

▶ The *Blinking Text* applet (page 56) randomly blinks words on and off, using different colors. It's eye-catching, but it can be hard to read.

▶ The *Nervous Text* applet (page 76) randomly jiggles the letters around in a line of displayed text.

▶ You can also display blinking, scrolling messages, as well as other effects, with a programmable *LED Sign* (page 68).

Business and Financial Applets

We've also included several applets that are useful for business documents and financial applications.

▶ The *Bar Chart* applet (page 51) displays a simple bar chart (shown here).

▶ Use the *Bar Graph* applet (page 53) to display and scroll through a larger or more complex data set.

▶ You can also display data with a *Line Graph* (page 70).

▶ You can even include a working, interactive *SpreadSheet* applet (page 81) to your Web page, to calculate your financial assets.

Demos, Games, and Educational Applets

Finally, we've included a collection of more involved applets that really show off Java's capabilities. These include games, simulations, and other amusing and educational applets.

Although these applets are too specialized to use in most Web pages, they are good as examples of what can be done with Java.

You can also try your hand at modifying these applets to create your own specialized applets. For example, you could modify the Crossword Puzzle applet to add your own puzzles, or you could change it to a different kind of word puzzle.

▶ Try the *Abacus* applet (page 46) to learn the ancient Chinese art of calculating with beads.

▶ You can shoot a cannon at a target with the *Ballistic Simulator* applet (page 50).

▶ The *Bouncing Heads* applet (page 57) features Jonathan Payne's disembodied head bouncing around the page.

▶ The interactive *Crossword Puzzle* (page 59) gives you feedback as you fill in the words.

▶ Our friends the *Dining Philosophers* (shown at left) illustrate a classic problem in computer science (page 60).

▶ You can create your own infinitely scrollable images with the *Escher Paint* applet (page 61).

▶ The *Graph Layout* applet (page 62) displays a graph that arranges itself on the page according to a heuristic algorithm.

▶ The *Neon Sign* applet (page 75) is simple yet attractive.

▶ The *Molecule Viewer* (page 73) helps you visualize molecules. You can rotate them with the mouse to see their structure.

▶ You can save the world from a meltdown with the *Nuclear Powerplant* applet (page 77).

▶ *Pythagoras' Theorem* (page 78) steps you through an animated proof.

▶ How about a game of *Tic-Tac-Toe* (page 83)?

▶ Experiment with the interactive *Voltage Circuit Simulator* (page 86).

The Sample Applet Description that follows shows you the general format for descriptions of the applets in this chapter.

SAMPLE APPLET DESCRIPTION

Features

Applet

Description

A description of the applet.

Parameters

The parameters that are specific to this applet. For simplicity, this list doesn't include the standard attributes such as width, height, code, etc. You specify these parameters using the <param> tag. See Chapter 3, "Applets Explained," on page 21 for details on how to specify applet parameters.

Example

An example of the applet tag for this applet. Put this tag in your Web page to embed the applet.

Formats

Formats used by this applet. This can be definitions of how to specify parameters or file formats used by the applet.

Comments

Any thoughts that we have on the applet.

Hints

Useful tips and tricks. This may be alternative uses of the applet, or it can point out cool features.

Author

The author of the applet.

LEGEND

Throughout this chapter, we've included icons to classify applets based on what features they have. For example, the Under Construction applet incorporates animation and audio.

 Animation   Mouse

 Audio   Keyboard

 Graphics   Text tricks

ABACUS

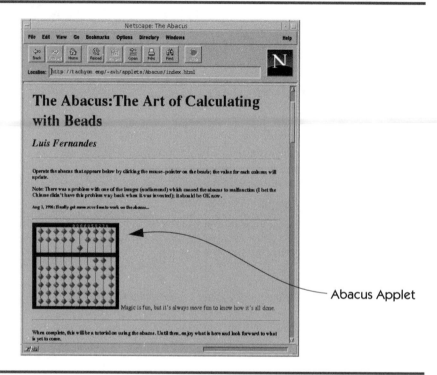

Abacus Applet

Description

The Abacus applet lets the user try out an abacus, an ancient Chinese calculator. The number entered into the abacus is displayed in the top edge of the applet.

Parameters

value   Initial value of the abacus. The beads will be set to this number, and the number will be displayed along the top edge of the abacus.

Example

```
<applet code="Abacus.class" width=210 height=200>
</applet>
```

Comments

This applet got an honorable mention in the alpha3 applet contest sponsored by the Java development team. It's a good example of how a simple applet can be used to illustrate concepts. In this case, the applet helps to explain an alternative way of calculating sums.

Author

Luis Fernandes

 http://www.ee.ryerson.ca:8080/~elf/

ANIMATOR

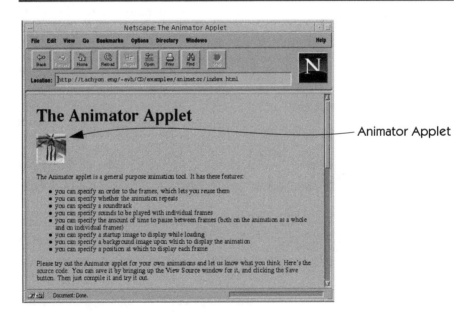

Animator Applet

Description

The Animator applet lets you create an animation with sound. You can specify a list of frames to be used to create the animation, whether the animation repeats, background audio, audio for individual frames, the position of each frame, and much more. The user clicks on the applet to stop the animation.

Clicking on the applet again restarts it. It's a more elaborate version of "ImageLoop" on page 64.

Parameters

imagesource	URL of the directory containing the images for the animation. The images are usually named T1.gif, T2.gif,...
startup	URL of an image that is displayed while downloading the rest of the frames.
background	URL of a background image.
startimage	Index of the first frame (usually 1).
endimage	Index of the last frame in the animation.
pause	Pause in milliseconds between each frame. This can be overridden by the pauses parameter.
pauses	List of pauses in milliseconds. This allows you to specify a different pause for each frame in the animation. Each number is separated by a | character. For example "200|0|100|100|...".
repeat	Repetition indicator. Use this to repeat the animation sequence. Can be either true or false (the default is true).
positions	The x@y positions of each frame. This lets you move the animation around. Each pair is separated by a | character. For example: "100@10|10@10|...".
images	Indexes of the images. This allows you to repeat frames of the animation. Each number is separated by a | character. For example: "1|2|3|2|1".
soundsource	URL of a directory containing the audio clips.
soundtrack	URL of an audio clip that is played repeatedly in the background (relative to the soundsource parameter).
sounds	List of URLs of audio clips that are played for each individual frame. The clips are separated by | characters. You can leave an entry empty if you want a moment of silence or if you don't want anything to be played by grouping two | characters together. For example: "tick.au||tock.au"

Example

```
<applet code=Animator.class width=64 height=64>
<param name=imagesource value="tower">
<param name=endimage value=2>
<param name=soundsource value="audio">
<param name=soundtrack value=spacemusic.au>
```

```
<param name=sounds value="1.au|2.au">
<param name=pause value=200>
</applet>
```

Author

Herb Jellinek, Sun Microsystems, Inc.

 http://www.javasoft.com/people/jellinek/

AUDIOITEM

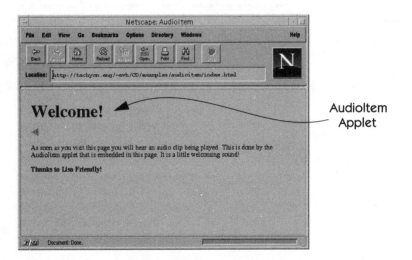

AudioItem
Applet

Description

The AudioItem applet plays an audio clip in a series of clips when a user accesses the Web page. Each time the page is visited, the next clip in the series is played. The user can also click on the applet's icon to play the next clip.

Parameters

snd   URLs of the audio clips that are to be played, separated by the
             | character.

Example

```
<applet code="AudioItem.class" width=15 height=15>
<param name=snd value="Hello.au|Welcome.au">
</applet>
```

Hints

This applet is useful for adding background music to a page. You can set the width and height to 0 if you don't want the icon to be visible.

Author

James Gosling, Sun Microsystems, Inc.

 http://www.javasoft.com/people/jag/

BALLISTIC SIMULATOR

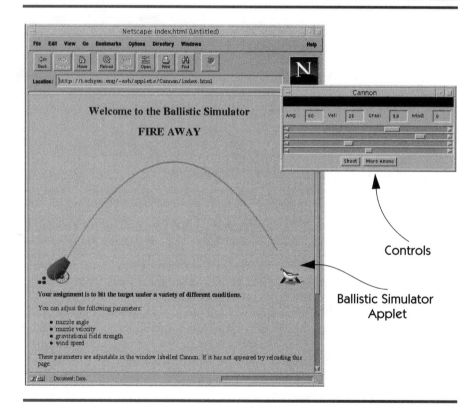

Controls

Ballistic Simulator
Applet

Description

The Ballistic Simulator applet lets you take shots at a fixed target with a cannon by setting the velocity and angle of the cannon, as well as the wind and gravity. This applet pops up an external window with controls for firing the cannon. The control window is only visible if you're on the page containing the applet.

Example

```
<applet code="cannon/cannon.class" width=600 height=300>
</applet>
```

Comments

This applet got an honorable mention in the alpha3 applet contest sponsored by the Java development team.

Author

Sean Russell

 http://guernsey.uoregon.edu/~ser/

BAR CHART

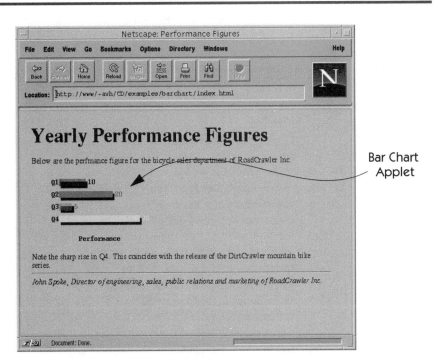

Bar Chart
Applet

Description

The Bar Chart applet displays a simple bar chart based on the parameters passed to the applet. The parameters that describe the bars are c1_style, c2_style, etc. See also the Bar Graph applet on page 53.

Parameters

title   Title of the bar chart. It is displayed below the graphics.

columns   Number of columns (bars) in the chart.

orientation   Position of the bar chart, which can be either horizontal or vertical.

scale   Number of pixels per unit in the bar graph.

c<N>_style   Appearance of the bars, which can be either solid or striped.

c<N>_value   Value of the bar (generally this is a quantity that can be measured—number of dollars, number of days, etc.).

c<N>_label   Label on the bar (generally this is what is being measured—money, time, etc.—or a time frame for the measurement).

c<N>_color   Color of the bar, either green, blue, pink, orange, magenta, cyan, white, yellow, gray, darkGray.

Example

```
<applet code="Chart.class" width=251 height=125>
<param name=title value="Performance">
<param name=columns value="4">
<param name=orientation value="horizontal">
<param name=scale value="5">
<param name=c1_style value="striped">
<param name=c1 value="10">
<param name=c1_color value="blue">
<param name=c1_label value="Q1">
<param name=c2_color value="green">
<param name=c2_label value="Q2">
<param name=c2 value="20">
<param name=c2_style value="solid">
<param name=c3 value="5">
<param name=c3_style value="striped">
<param name=c3_color value="magenta">
```

```
<param name=c3_label value="Q3">
<param name=c4 value="30">
<param name=c4_color value="yellow">
<param name=c4_label value="Q4">
<param name=c4_style value="solid">
</applet>
```

Hints

Try setting the orientation parameter to vertical. Remember to choose a width and height big enough so that the entire chart fits in the applet area.

Comments

The user can't interact with the bar chart. It's for display only.

Author

Sami Shaio, Sun Microsystems, Inc.

 http://www.javasoft.com/people/sami/

Bar Graph

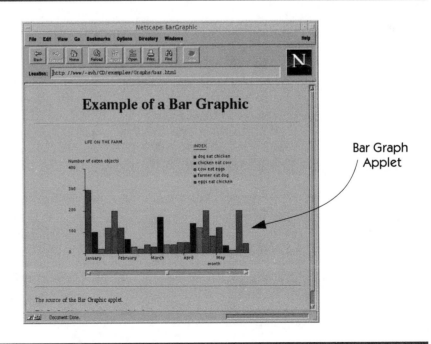

Bar Graph Applet

Description

The Bar Graph applet displays a bar graph that has multiple data sets. The graph contains a horizontal scrollbar, so the data can be wider than the page. See also Line Graph on page 70 and Bar Chart on page 51.

Parameters

filename	URL of the file containing the graph data (see below).
dir	URL of the directory containing the data files named by the filename parameter.
header	Title of the graph.
xtext	Title of the x axis.
ytext	Title of the y axis.
vybegin	First value of the y axis.
vygap	Unit width on the y axis.
xgap	Width in pixels of a unit on the x axis.
ygap	Width in pixels of the unit width specified in the vygap parameter.

Example

```
<applet code="BarApplet.class" width=499 height=370>
<param name=filename value="bars.data">
<param name=dir value="dataFiles/">
<param name=header value="LIFE ON THE FARM">
<param name=xtext value="month">
<param name=ytext value="Number of eaten objects">
<param name=vybegin value="0">
<param name=vygap value="100">
<param name=xgap value="80">
<param name=ygap value="50">
</applet>
```

File Format

The file format is fairly simple. It starts with a description of the x-axis units and is followed by a number of data sets. Each data set consists of a title, a color, and a set of comma-separated values. Lines starting with # are ignored. For example:

```
# number of Units
9
```

```
# units
January
February
March
April
May
June
July
August
September

# number of data sets
5

# the name of the first data set
dog eat chicken
# color
255, 0, 0

# values
300, 120, 30, 50,120,250,50,30,60

chicken eat cow
0, 0, 255
100, 67, 170, 140,34,50,120,300,350

cow eat eggs
0,255,0
20, 30, 40, 120,12,123,320,150,45

farmer eat dog
204, 0, 204
120, 20, 40, 200,200,40,250,60,32

eggs eat chicken
0, 204, 0
200, 40, 50, 80,45,120,40,56,340
```

Author

Siebe Brouwer, HIO Enschede, Holland.

 http://www.javasoft.com/people/siebe/

BLINKING TEXT

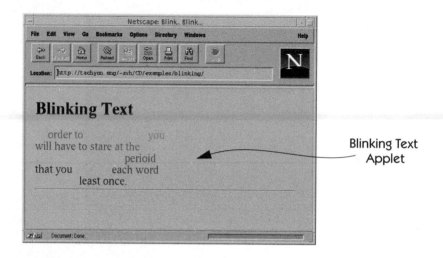

Blinking Text Applet

Description

The Blinking Text applet displays a paragraph of text and randomly shows and hides words in different colors.

Parameters

speed   The number of times per second that the text blinks. Set this to a value between 1 and 10.

lbl   The text displayed inside the applet.

Example

```
<applet code="Blink.class" width=300 height=100>
<param name=lbl value="This is the next best thing to sliced bread!">
<param name=speed value=4>
</applet>
```

Comments

The blinking aspect makes for an interesting show, but the text itself is hard to read. The blink applet was created as a joke, to parody Netscape's infamous <blink> tag.

Hints

You need to vary the width and height of the applet so all text fits.

Author

Arthur van Hoff, Sun Microsystems, Inc.

 http://www.javasoft.com/people/avh/

BOUNCING HEADS

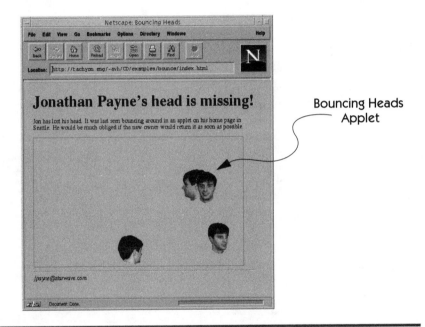

Bouncing Heads
Applet

Description

The Bouncing Heads applet displays a number of bouncing and rotating images. The bouncing is influenced by simulated gravity and friction.

Example

```
<applet codebase=BouncingHeads code="BounceItem.class"
     width=500 height=300>
</applet>
```

Comments

This applet is mostly for entertainment, and it has no useful parameters that you can configure. Jonathan Payne, who wrote this applet, was the original author of HotJava. This applet was one of the first that he wrote for HotJava to demonstrate Java's animation and audio features.

Author

Jonathan Payne, Starwave Inc., Seattle

    http://www.starwave.com/people/jpayne/

CLOCK

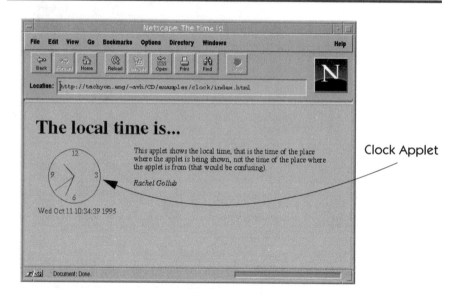

Clock Applet

Description

The Clock applet displays an analog clock that has a second hand and the date below the clock face. The time that is shown is the time local to the person who is viewing the page.

Example

```
<applet code="Clock2.class" width=170 height=150>
</applet>
```

Author

Rachel Gollub, Sun Microsystems, Inc.

 http://www.javasoft.com/people/rmg/

CROSSWORD PUZZLE

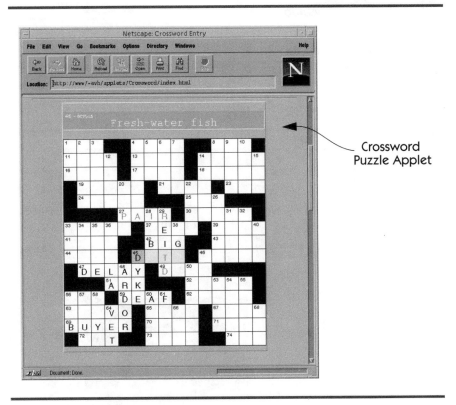

Crossword
Puzzle Applet

Description

The Crossword Puzzle applet is interactive. The user can select a position and enter a word. Correct letters are displayed in black; incorrect letters are rendered in red.

Example

```
<applet code="crossword.class" width=455 height=543>
</applet>
```

Comments

This applet got an honorable mention in the alpha3 applet contest sponsored by the Java development team. It is an example of an applet that is automatically generated by a program. The program to generate the puzzle code is not included on the CD-ROM.

Author

Carl W. Haynes III, Software Engineer, Starwave Corporation, WA.

 http://www.starwave.com/people/haynes/

DINING PHILOSOPHERS

Dining
Philosophers
Applet

Description

The Dining Philosophers applet is an animated demonstration of the classic multi-processing synchronization problem in computer science. The applets show five philosophers that either talk, eat, or wait. There are four audio settings, and sliders are provided to control how talkative, hungry, and patient the philosophers are.

Example

```
<applet code="DiningPhilosphers.class" width=440 height=550>
</applet>
```

Comments

This applet won the first prize in the alpha3 applet contest sponsored by the Java development team. It was selected for excellent use of animation and audio. A very funny applet.

Author

Brian Gloyer, graduate student in electrical and computer engineering, UC, Irvine.

 http://www.eng.uci.edu/~bgloyer/

ESCHER PAINT

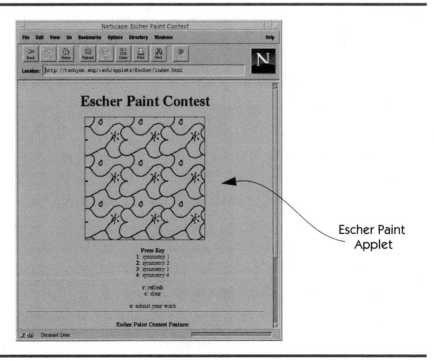

Escher Paint Applet

Description

The Escher Paint applet lets the user design symmetric paintings in the style of M.C. Escher. Each line that is drawn is repeated several times, for a kaleido-scope effect. The user can select various symmetries.

Example

```
<applet code="escherpaint.class" width=300 height=300>
</applet>
```

Comments

This applet got an honorable mention in the alpha3 applet contest sponsored by the Java development team. It's a good example of an interactive painting applet.

Author

Yoshiaki Araki

 http://www.sfc.keio.ac.jp/~t93827ya/

GRAPH LAYOUT

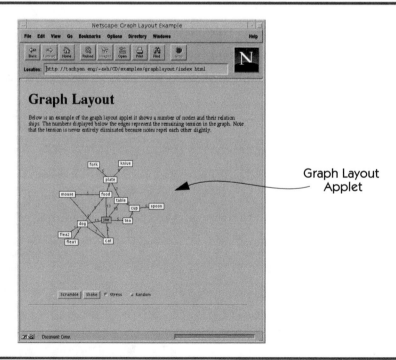

Graph Layout Applet

Description

The Graph Layout applet dynamically displays a graph consisting of nodes and arcs. The algorithm used to lay out the graph is heuristic, and it slowly attempts to optimize the tension in the arcs of the graph. The nodes repel each either slightly to space the nodes. You can define which nodes are used, as well as the optimal length of the edges between them.

Parameters

center   The center node of the graph. This node will be fixed to the center of the screen. This node is displayed in red.

edges   The edges of the graph. See below for an explanation of the format.

Example

```
<applet code="Graph.class" width=400 height=400>
<param name=edges value="joe-food,joe-dog,joe-tea,
   joe-cat,joe-table,table-plate/50,plate-food/30,
   food-mouse/100,food-dog/100,mouse-cat/150,table-cup/30,
   cup-tea/30,dog-cat/80,cup-spoon/50,plate-fork,
   dog-flea1,dog-flea2,flea1-flea2/20,plate-knife">
<param name=center value="joe">
</applet>
```

Formats

The format of the edges parameter consists of a comma-separated list of edges between nodes. The nodes are created as they're needed. Each edge is defined as a pair of nodes:

```
<from>-<to>
```

You can also specify the desired length of the edge:

```
<from>-<to>/<length>
```

Hints

Choosing the length of the edges defines how closely related the <from> and <to> nodes are.

Comments

The user can pick up nodes and distort the graph to speed up the layout process.

Author

Arthur van Hoff, Sun Microsystems, Inc.

 http://www.javasoft.com/people/avh/

IMAGELOOP

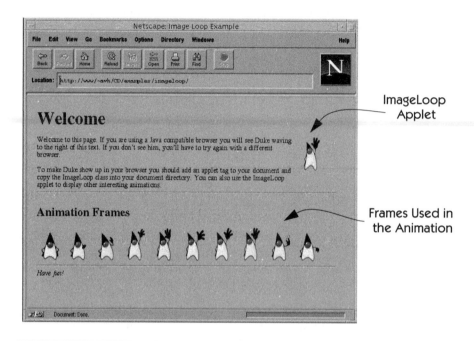

ImageLoop
Applet

Frames Used in
the Animation

Description

The ImageLoop applet plays a sequence of images repeatedly to create animation. You need to supply a list of images for the animation. The user can click on the animation to stop it. The animation starts again when the user leaves the page and then comes back, or when the user clicks on the animation a second time. To add sound to your animation, take a look at the Animator applet on page 47.

Parameters

img   Specifies the URL where the images should be loaded for the animation. This URL should eventually point to the location of a directory that contains the images. The naming convention for the images is: T1.gif... T<N>.gif.

nimgs   Number of images in the animation.

pause   A pause in milliseconds between animations. The animation will halt for this length of time on the first frame of the animation.

Comments

This is a good way to add more sparkle to your logo or to draw the user's attention to a particular section of your document.

Example

```
<applet code=ImageLoopItem width=80 height=90 align=right>
<param name=nimgs value=10>
<param name=img value=duke>
<param name=pause value=1000>
</applet>
```

Author

James Gosling, Sun Microsystems, Inc.

 http://www.javasoft.com/people/jag/

IMAGEMAP

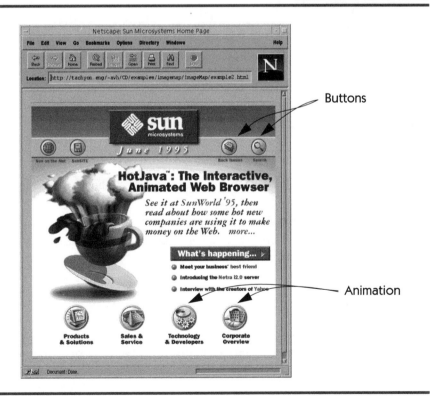

Buttons

Animation

Description

The ImageMap applet is used to create client-side image maps that are interactive and offer direct feedback. (As you probably know, an image map is an image that has active areas that the user can select and/or click on.) The active areas of the image map defined in the applet parameters can be given various extensible behaviors such as sounds effects, animations, hyper links, highlights, etc.

Parameters

img   URL of the background image.

highlight   Type of highlighting that should be used. Use either `brighter<N>` or `darker<N>`, where N is a percentage. For example, `brighter20`.

startsound   URL of an audio file that is played as soon as the applet starts.

area<N>   Defines an active area of the image. Each applet can have one or more of these areas. The format of this value is defined below.

Example

```
<applet codebase=ImageMap code="ImageMap.class"
     width=421 height=277>
<param name=img value=trix.gif>
<param name=highlight value=brighter20>
<param name=area1 value="HighlightArea,262,96,104,135,darker20">
<param name=area2 value="SoundArea,10,40,401,207,drip.au">
<param name=area3 value="HighlightArea,10,40,401,207">
<param name=area4 value="ClickArea,0,0,421,277">
</applet>
```

The example defines a simple image map containing several active areas.

Formats

Each area<n> parameter defines a rectangular area in the background image. Each area has the following format:

    class,x,y,width,height,arguments...

The class component defines the type of area that is to be used, and the x, y, width, and height components define the coordinates of the affected area in the image. Each type of area can have additional arguments.

SoundArea	Plays an audio clip when the mouse enters the area. It takes the URL of the audio clip as an additional argument.
Delayed-SoundArea	Plays an audio clip when the mouse stays in the area for a minimum amount of time. It takes the URL of the audio clip and an amount of time in milliseconds as additional arguments.
LinkArea	Goes to a URL when the user clicks in this area. It takes the target URL as an argument.
NameArea	Shows a string in the status line of the browser when the mouse enters the area. It takes a string as an argument.
HRef-ButtonArea	Goes to a URL when the user clicks in this area. It also displays a button border when the mouse enters this area.
RoundHref-ButtonArea	Goes to a URL when the user clicks in this area. It also displays a circular button border when the mouse enters this area
Highlight-Area	Highlights the area when the mouse enters. It takes an optional argument, which is the percentage of highlighting required (see the highlight parameter).
AniArea	Plays an animation when the mouse enters the area. It takes the URL of an image containing several frames of an animation (a strip) and a list of x, y coordinates defining the location of the individual frames in the strip.
ClickArea	Displays the coordinates when the user clicks in this area. It's mostly used during debugging.

Note that the various effects are defined by simple Java classes that are dynamically loaded when needed. You can define your own subclass of class ImageMapArea. Check out the code for more information on how to do this.

Comments

The ImageMap applet is an extremely useful applet that can be configured in many different ways to create interesting image maps.

Note that the image map can contain overlapping areas, and the input to areas is processed in order. So if you want to specify areas that are nested, you should specify the innermost area first.

Hints

When creating an ImageMap applet, add a `ClickArea` that covers the entire image (as shown in the example). This way you can select areas of the image with your mouse, and the coordinates will be displayed in the status line of your browser. You can then edit the applet tag and add an area that corresponds to the coordinates that you've selected.

Author

Jim Graham, Sun Microsystems, Inc.

 http://www.javasoft.com/people/flar/

LED SIGN

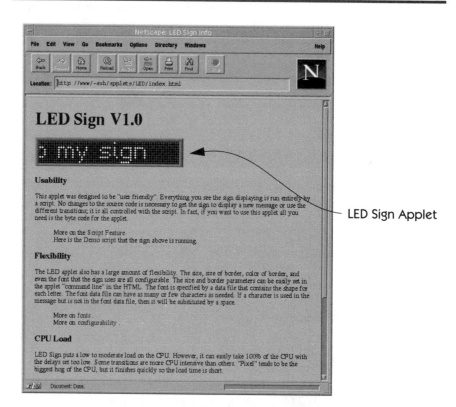

LED Sign Applet

Description

The LED[1] Sign applet can be programmed using an elaborate scripting language to perform a wide range of displays including scrolling, flashing, colors, special effects, etc.

Parameters

script   Name of the file containing the script that controls the LED sign.

font   Name of the font description file. This is usually fonts/default.font.

spacewidth   Width of a space.

bordercolor   Color of the border. This should be three numbers between 0 and 255 separated by commas.

border   Width of the border.

Example

```
<applet code="LED/LED.class" width=320 height=60>
<param name=script value="scripts/Demo.led">
<param name=font value="fonts/default.font">
<param name=spacewidth value="3">
<param name=bordercolor value="100,130,130">
<param name=border value="3">
</applet>
```

Comments

This applet got a shared third prize in the alpha3 applet contest sponsored by the Java development team. A description of the scripting language that is used to control the LED display is included on the CD-ROM.

Author

Darrick Brown, undergraduate student, Computer Science, Hope College, Holland, MI.

 http://www.cs.hope.edu/~dbrown/

---

[1] Light Emitting Diodes

LINE GRAPH

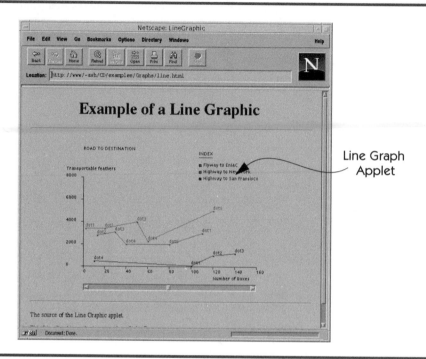

Description

The Line Graph applet displays a line graph with multiple data sets. The graph contains a horizontal scrollbar so that the data can be wider than the page. See also the Bar Graph applet on page 53.

Parameters

filename	URL of the file containing the graph data (see File Format section following).
dir	URL of the directory containing the data files named by the filename parameter.
header	Title of the graph.
xtext	Title of the x axis.
ytext	Title of the y axis.
vybegin	First value of the y axis.
vxgap	Unit width on the x axis.

vygap   Unit width on the y axis.

xgap   Width in pixels of the unit width specified in the vxgap parameter.

ygap   Width in pixels of the unit width specified in the vygap parameter.

Example

```
<applet code=TestDiagram.class width=500 height=370>
<param name=filename value="lines.data">
<param name=dir value="dataFiles/">
<param name=header value="ROAD TO DESTINATION">
<param name=xtext value="Number of Boxes">
<param name=ytext value="Transportable feathers">
<param name=vxbegin value="0">
<param name=vxgap value="20">
<param name=vybegin value="0">
<param name=vygap value="2000">
<param name=xgap value="50">
<param name=ygap value="50">
</applet>
```

File Format

The file format is fairly simple and describes the data sets in turn. Each data set consists of a title, a color, and a set of values. Each value consists of a name, x, and y value. Lines starting with # are ignored. For example:

```
# number of data sets
3

# the name of the data set
Flyway to EniaC

# color
255,0,0

# data points
5
dot1, 110, 3000
dot2, 13, 2800
dot3, 30, 3100
dot4, 40, 2000
dot5, 80, 2000
Highway to New York
204, 0, 204
5
```

```
dot1, 2, 3400
dot2, 20, 3400
dot3, 50, 4000
dot4, 60, 2300
dot5, 120, 5000

Highway to San Francisco
0 , 0, 255
4
dot1, 100, 100
dot2, 120, 1000
dot3, 140, 1200
dot4, 10, 500
```

Author

Siebe Brouwer, HIO Enschede, Holland.

 http://www.javasoft.com/people/siebe/

LINK BUTTON

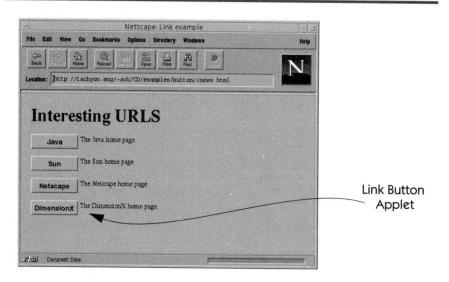

Link Button Applet

Description

The Link Button applet lets you put a button in a Web page. When the button is clicked, a new page is shown. An audio clip can also be played when the button is clicked.

Parameters

href   URL of the document to which the user goes when the button is
          clicked. This URL can be relative to the current document.

snd   URL of an audio clip that is played when the button is clicked.

Example

```
<applet code=LinkButton.java width=100 height=30>
<param name=lbl value="Java">
<param name=href value="http://www.javasoft.com/">
<param name=snd value="computer.au">
</applet>
```

Author

Arthur van Hoff, Sun Microsystems, Inc.

   http://www.javasoft.com/people/avh/

MOLECULE VIEWER

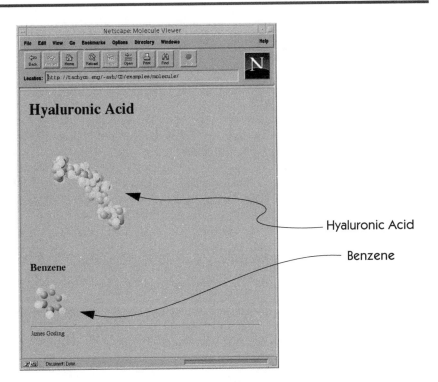

Description

The Molecule Viewer applet displays a molecule and lets the user rotate it to any desired angle. The molecule is rendered in real time, and it may consist of many different atoms. Each atom is displayed with the appropriate depth clues.

Parameters

model
: URL of the file containing the description of the molecule that will be displayed. Note that this can be an absolute URL or the name of a file relative to the document in which the applet is located.

scale
: Optional scale factor. This lets you to scale the display ot the molecule by a floating point factor. Use values between 0.5 and 4.0.

Example

```
<applet code="XYZApp.class" width=300 height=300>
<param name=model value="models/HyaluronicAcid.xyz">
</applet>
```

Formats

The molecule is defined in the file referred to by the model parameter. The format of this file, which is really simple, is an atom description per line, with each atom having the form:

```
ELEMENT X-POS Y-POS Z-POS
```

The element can be one of the following: C, H, N, O. The X, Y, and Z coordinates usually range from -1.0 to 1.0, but the scale can be adjusted using the scale parameter. Here is an example of the description of a benzene molecule:

```
C 0.0998334 0.995004 0
H 0.159733 1.59201 0
C 0.911616 0.411044 0
H 1.45859 0.65767 0
C 0.811782 -0.58396 0
H 1.29885 -0.934337 0
C -0.0998334 -0.995004 0
H -0.159733 -1.59201 0
C -0.911616 -0.411044 0
H -1.45858 -0.65767 0
C -0.811782 0.583961 0
H -1.29885 0.934337 0
```

Comment

This applet is an excellent example of how Java can be used for educational purposes. It is helpful to be able to rotate the molecules in order to get a feeling for their shape.

It also shows how to achieve a powerful illusion of 3D graphics in Java using 3D projection and progressively smaller images of individual spheres.

Author

James Gosling, Sun Microsystems, Inc.

 http://www.javasoft.com/people/jag/

NEON SIGN

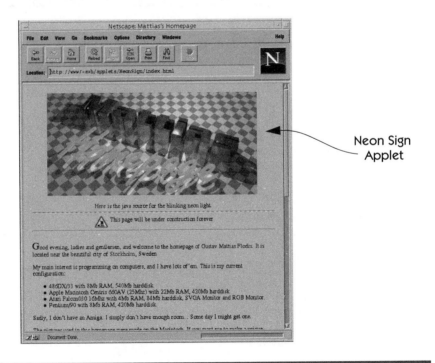

Neon Sign
Applet

Description

The Neon Sign applet is quite flashy—literally. If your first name is Mattias, you'll love this applet.

Example

```
<applet code="BlinkItem.class" width=512 height=243>
</applet>
```

Comments

This applet got an honorable mention in the alpha3 applet contest sponsored by the Java development team. It is an example of a simple applet that creates an interesting effect by randomly alternating two images.

Author

Mattias Flodin, undergraduate in natural sciences, Rudbecksskolan Gymnasium.

http://www.rbk.sollentuna.se/~mfl_94/

NERVOUS TEXT

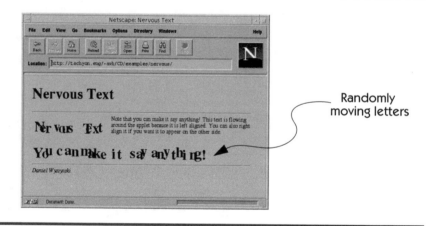

Randomly moving letters

Description

The Nervous Text applet displays a single line of text and randomly moves the letters around. It's a surprisingly popular applet. The effect is simple, but very effective.

Parameters

text   The text displayed in this applet. The applet can display only one line of text.

Example

```
<applet code="NervousText.class" width=200 height=50>
<param name=text value="Hello World!">
</applet>
```

Hints

You need to pick the width of the applet so that it fits the entire string.

Comments

This applet is often used to spice up a Web page. It is also useful as a signature in mail or news messages—but only those viewing the messages with a Hot-Java browser will get the effect.

Author

Daniel Wyszynski

 http://forte.poly.edu:8000/

NUCLEAR POWERPLANT

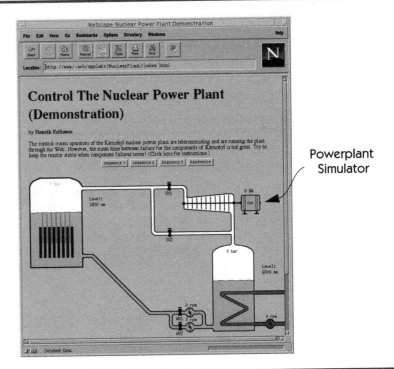

Powerplant
Simulator

Description

The Nuclear Powerplant applet is an interesting simulation and a game of sorts. The applet simulates the operation of a powerplant, with a little danger mixed in. Users can choose from three different disaster scenarios and then try to beat the clock to save the powerplant from a meltdown by turning off pumps, opening and closing valves, and lowering and raising fuel rods.

Example

```
<applet code="NuclearPlant.class" width=680 height=473>
</applet>
```

Comments

This applet got the second prize in the alpha3 applet contest sponsored by the Java development team. It was selected for excellent use of graphics, animation, and audio. All the valves, pumps, and rods can be operated by the user. If the user fails to operate the powerplant correctly, a meltdown may result.

Hints

The applet is a little wider than a normal page, so you will have to resize the browser window to see the entire applet.

Author

Henrik Eriksson, Ph.D., Assistant Professor, Dept. of Computer and Information Science, Linköping University, Sweden.

 http://www.ida.liu.se/~her/

PYTHAGORAS' THEOREM   

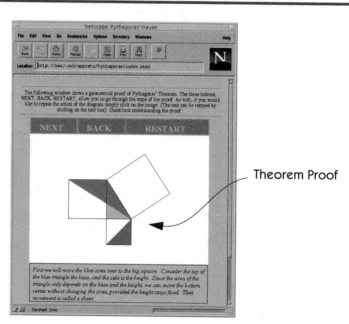

Theorem Proof

Description

The Pythagoras's Theorem applet is an animated, step-by-step explanation of that famous geometric proof, in which the square of the hypotenuse of a right angle triangle is equal to the sum of the squares of the other two sides. It uses numerous interesting animated text effects.

Parameters

pause   Pause, in milliseconds, between animations.

Example

```
<applet code=Pythagoras.class width=500 height=500>
<param name=pause value=0>
</applet>
```

Comments

This applet was the grand-prize winner of the alpha3 applet contest sponsored by the Java development team. It was selected for its educational value and its excellent use of Java. It also implemented a triangle-fill operation, a functionality that the alpha3 API did not provide.

Author

Jim Morey, Department of Mathematics, University of British Columbia, Canada

 http://www.math.ubc.ca/~morey/morey.html

SCROLLING IMAGES

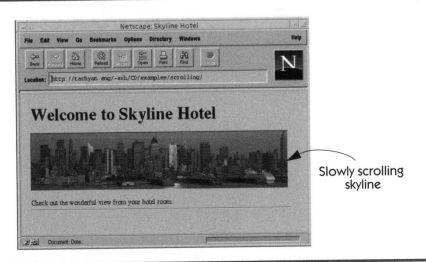

Slowly scrolling skyline

Description

The Scrolling Images applet displays one or more images and scrolls them either to the left or to the right of the screen. The images are displayed incrementally as they are being downloaded.

Parameters

speed   Number of times per second that the images will be scrolled.

dir   Direction (in pixels) in which the images will be scrolled in each frame. Use a number between 1 and 10 to scroll to right, and a number between -1 and -10 to scroll to the left.

nimgs   Number of images to be displayed.

img   URL of the directory containing the images. The naming convention for the images is T1.gif, T2.gif,...

Example

```
<applet code="ImageTape.class" width=550 height=50>
<param name=speed value=4>
<param name=img value="images/team">
<param name=dir value=4>
<param name=nimgs value="15">
</applet>
```

The example makes some of the members of the Java team scroll by to the right. There are 15 images that are scrolled 4 pixels, 4 times per second (that means a total of 16 pixels per second).

Comments

This applet can be used to display a large number of images incrementally or an image that is too wide for the page. It's a good way to show panoramic images.

Hints

Make sure that all the images are about the same height.

Author

Arthur van Hoff, Sun Microsystems, Inc.

http://www.javasoft.com/people/avh/

SPREADSHEET

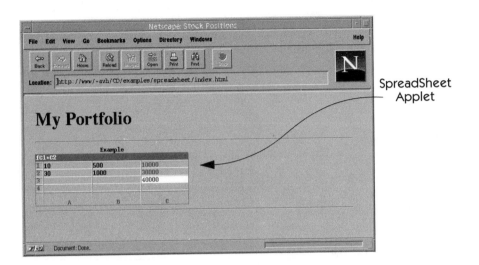

SpreadSheet
Applet

Description

The SpreadSheet applet is a simple spreadsheet application that visitors to your Web site can use. You can define the contents of the cells by setting the applet parameters. The user can select cells, enter new values, and edit existing values. Cells can contain strings, values, or formulas.

Parameters

title   Title for the spreadsheet.

rows   Number of rows in the spreadsheet.

colums   Number of columns in the spreadsheet.

<C><R>   Value of the spreadsheet cell at the given column (a letter from A to Z) and the given row (a number between 1 and the number of rows). For example, the name of the 2nd column and the first row would be B1. The values of the cells are explained below.

Example

```
<applet code="SpreadSheet.class" width=320 height=120>
<param name=title value="Example">
```

```
<param name=rows value="4">
<param name=cols value="3">
<param name=A1 value="v10">
<param name=A2 value="v30">
<param name=B1 value="v500">
<param name=B2 value="v1000">
<param name=C1 value="fA1*B2">
<param name=C2 value="fA2*B2">
<param name=C3 value="fC1+C2">
</applet>
```

Formats

Each cell in the spreadsheet can have either a string label, a numeric value, or a formula. Use l<label> as the value of the cell for a label; v<value> for numeric constants, and f<formula> formulas. A formula can contain the following operations:

```
Value + Value
Value - Value
Value * Value
Value / Value
```

Each value in an expression can be the value of another cell in the spreadsheet, a numeric constant, or another formula wrapped inside parentheses. For example, the value of this formula is 100 plus contents of cell A1:

```
A1 + 100
```

Here is a more complex example of a formula:

```
A1 + (B3 * 100)
```

Comments

The values of the cells are computed from the uppermost left corner down. This means that in order for formulas to work correctly, they should not contain references to cells that are to the right and below the current cell.

Author

Sami Shaio, Sun Microsystems, Inc.

   http://www.javasoft.com/people/sami/

Tic-Tac-Toe

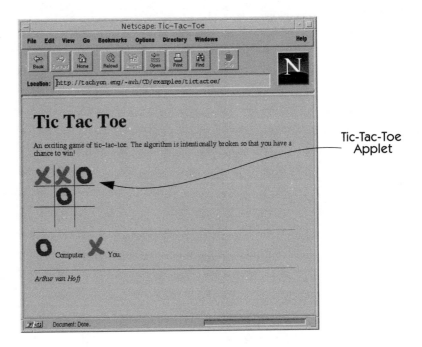

Tic-Tac-Toe
Applet

Description

The Tic-Tac-Toe applet is a simple game of tic-tac-toe that can be played on your Web pages. The algorithm is intentionally broken to give the user a chance to win. Click on a square to make the first move.

Example

```
<applet code="TicTacToe.class" width=120 height=120>
</applet>
```

Author

Arthur van Hoff, Sun Microsystems, Inc.

    http://www.javasoft.com/people/avh/

TUMBLING DUKE

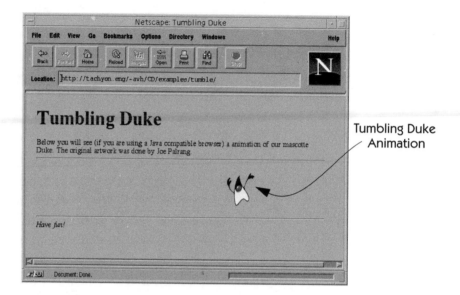

Tumbling Duke Animation

Description

The Tumbling Duke applet shows Duke tumbling. The animation consists of 17 frames.

Parameters

maxwidth   Width of the widest image in the animation.

nimgs   Number of frames in the animation.

offset   Horizontal offset between the last and the first frame of the animation.

img   URL of a directory containing the animation frames which follow the naming convention of T1.gif, T2.gif, ...

Example

```
<applet code="TumbleItem.class" width=600 height=95>
<param name=maxwidth value="120">
<param name=nimgs value="16">
<param name=offset value="-57">
<param name=img value="tumble">
</applet>
```

Author

Arthur van Hoff, Sun Microsystems, Inc.

 http://www.javasoft.com/people/avh/

UNDER CONSTRUCTION

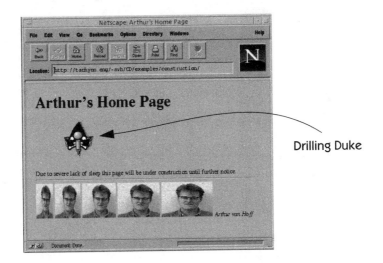

Drilling Duke

Description

The Under Construction applet displays an animated under-construction sign featuring Duke.

Example

```
<applet code="JackhammerDuke.class" width=300 height=300>
</applet>
```

Hints

Duke will randomly slide to the left and to the right. Therefore it's best to make the applet fairly wide.

Author

Bob Weisblat, Sun Microsystems, Inc.

 http://www.javasoft.com/people/weisblat/

VOLTAGE CIRCUIT SIMULATOR

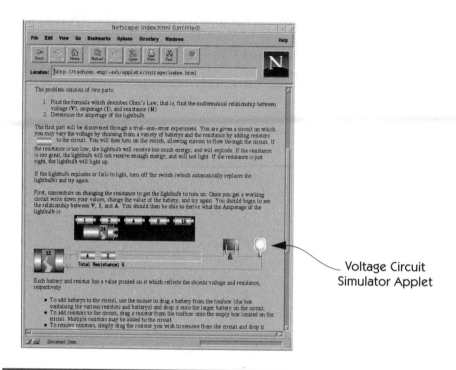

Voltage Circuit
Simulator Applet

Description

This educational applet lets students discover the relationship between voltage, amperage, and resistance. The user can position resistors, replace the battery, and turn on the light. The light will only come on if the correct resistors have been added to the circuit.

Example

```
<applet code="voltage/voltage.class" width=600 height=150>
</applet>
```

Comments

This applet got an honorable mention in the alpha3 applet contest sponsored by the Java development team. It is an excellent example of an educational applet.

Author

Sean Russell

 http://guernsey.uoregon.edu/~ser/

WHAT'S NEW!

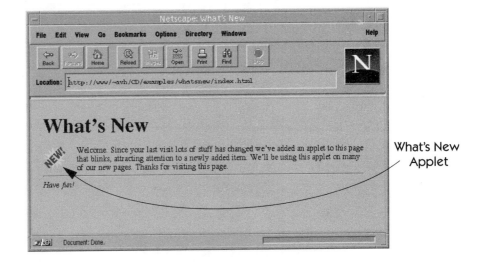

What's New
Applet

Description

The What's New applet displays an animated logo. It can be used to attract attention to a new portion of a Web page.

Example

```
<applet code="WhatsNew.class" width=40 height=40>
</applet>
```

Hints

The width and height of the applet control the scale of the image. That means you can make it smaller than in the above example.

Author

Arthur van Hoff, Sun Microsystems, Inc.

 http://www.javasoft.com/people/avh/

WIRE FRAME VIEWER

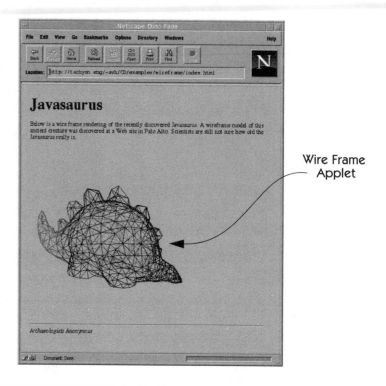

Wire Frame
Applet

Description

The Wire Frame applet displays a wire frame model rendered in real time, with limited depth cues, and the option of many edges. The user can rotate the model to any desired angle.

Parameters

model   URL of the file containing the description of the wire frame
            model that will be displayed.

scale   Optional scale factor that controls the overall scaling of the
            model. Uses values between 0.5 and 4.0.

Example

```
<applet codebase=WireFrame code="ThreeD.class"
    width=400 height=400>
<param name=model value="WireFrame/models/dinasaur.obj">
<param name=scale value="1.4">
</applet>
```

Formats

The format used by this applet is the WaveFront .obj format. It's such a simple
format that you can create models with a text editor. Here's what the definition of a simple cube looks like:

```
v 0 0 0
v 1 0 0
v 1 1 0
v 0 1 0
v 0 0 1
v 1 0 1
v 1 1 1
v 0 1 1
f 1 2 3 4
f 5 6 7 8
l 1 5
l 2 6
l 3 7
l 4 8
```

Input lines starting with v define an x, y, z coordinate. Input lines starting
with f or l define an edge or a set of edges.

Author

James Gosling, Sun Microsystems, Inc.

    http://www.javasoft.com/people/jag/

ZINE

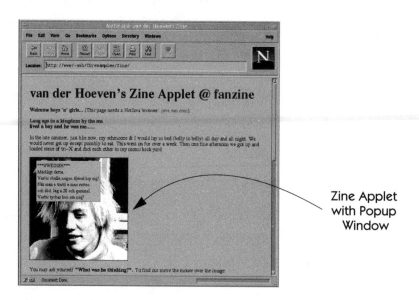

Zine Applet
with Popup
Window

Description

The Zine applet displays an image. As the user moves the mouse over different areas of the image, popup windows with text appear. With this feature, you can annotate an image or create a text-balloon effect like you might find in a comic strip.

Parameters

dataurl   URL of the data file describing the active areas of the image and the text of the popups.

imgurl   URL of the background image.

showhot   Shows all active areas if set to yes. This parameter is useful when creating the applet.

Example

```
<applet code="Zine.class" width=275 height=278>
<param name=dataurl value="jojo.zine">
<param name=imgurl value="JOJOMD.GIF">
</applet>
```

Formats

The format of the data files that describes the active areas is fairly simple: the point (x, y) where the popup window is shown on the image and a rect (x, y, width, height) that describes the active area is enclosed in curly braces. The file must also contain strings in double quotes, one for each line of text in the popup window. Lines starting with a # character are ignored. For example:

```
{
    #point:
    20 120
    #rect:
    14 14 260 139
    #text:
    "***ENGLISH***"
    "It is real strange to be here."
    "Why would anyone care what I think?"
    "When you are thirty you are rotten"
    "and you die. I´m twenty and I´m old."
    "Why does she like me?"
}
{
    #point:
    20 120
    #rect:
    14 140 260 262
    #text:
    "***SWEDISH***"
    "Markligt detta."
    "Varfor skulle nagon djavel bry sig?"
    "Nor man e tretti e man rutten"
    "och dod. Jag e 20 och gammal."
    "Varfor tycker hon om mig?"
}
```

Comments

This is an extremely useful applet for highlighting the content of images. It can be used to name the people in a image or it can be used to create comic strips or comic books.

Author

Johan van der Hoeven

 http://www.fanzine.se/java/jo/

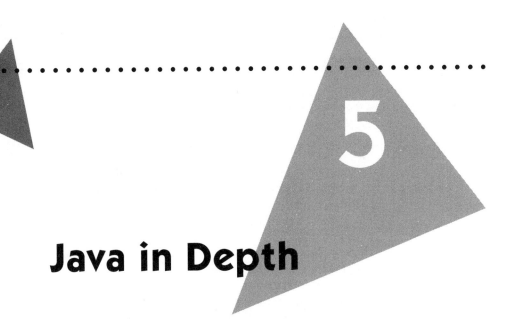

Java in Depth

The previous chapters introduced you to Java and showed you to how to use Java applets in your HTML pages. This chapter covers some of the major features of the Java language. The next chapter will build on this one and provide hands-on experience in building your own applets.

In order to take advantage of this chapter, you should have some experience programming with the C language. Whenever possible, Java uses C syntax because many programmers are familiar with it. Experience with C++ would also be useful, but it's not required to understand the material in this chapter. Even if you're familiar with object-oriented programming, it'll be worthwhile to review this chapter since Java has a different (and much simpler) set of object concepts than C++.

HELLO WORLD

In this section, we'll describe some general properties of the language and give you a simple example (Listing 5.1) that shows the mechanics of compiling and running a Java program.

LISTING 5.1 Hello World example

```
1:  /*
2:   * File: HelloWorld.java
3:   */
```

```
4:  public class HelloWorld {
5:    public static void main(String args[]) {
6:      System.out.println("Hello World");
7:    }
8:  }
```

If you have experience with C++, then this example might seem somewhat familiar. Otherwise, don't worry. The rest of the chapter will explain the language in much more detail.

Java is a statically compiled language, which means that Listing 5.1 must be compiled before it can be run. As a point of interest, the Java compiler is also written in Java, so it will run without any changes on all the platforms that support Java.

The CD-ROM included with this book has instructions on how to install the Java runtime system on your computer so you can run the examples. To compile the example, run the javac program, which is actually the Java compiler:

```
javac HelloWorld.java
```

This command will produce a file called HelloWorld.class, which contains translated instructions called byte-codes. They can be run by a Java interpreter on any platform that supports the interpreter, because they are in a platform-independent format. In order to run the example, pass in the name of the class we compiled to the Java interpreter:

```
java HelloWorld
```

If all went well, this will print out "Hello World" on your screen.

OVERVIEW OF JAVA SYNTAX

Java's syntax is very similar to C, to make the language more accessible to people already familiar with C or C++. However, there are some differences that are worthy of mention. This section goes over some of those differences and gives a whirlwind tour of the language's syntax. A more exhaustive account of the Java language can be found in the language spec at the Java Web site.

     http://www.javasoft.com/hooked/language-ref.html

Comments

Java combines the comment syntax for both C and C++. It also has a syntax that can be used to generate formatted documentation automatically:

```
/* same as C, comment characters don't nest */

// comment to the end of the line
/** "doc" comment. Can be used to generate documentation
    but must only be placed before a declaration. */
```

Basic Types

All of the simple types in Java are defined in the same way in all implementations of the language, independent of platform. This makes Java programs more portable than programs in C and C++. Here is the set of simple types supported by the language:

`boolean`   A true or false value. There is no conversion between booleans and any of the other simple types.

`byte`   8-bit signed quantity

`short`   16-bit signed quantity

`char`   16-bit Unicode character

`int`   32-bit signed quantity

`float`   32-bit IEEE754 floating-point

`double`   64-bit IEEE754 floating-point

`long`   64-bit signed quantity

Arrays

Support and syntax for arrays is much the same in Java as it is in C. However, Java does not allow arrays to be allocated on the stack, so they have to be allocated dynamically. Below are a few examples of array declarations.

```
// a single-dimensional array of ints
int    numbers[] = new int[10];
int[]    numbers = new int[10];

// a two-dimensional array of ints
int    matrix[][] = new int[5][10];
int[][] matrix = new int[5][10];

// initializing an array explicitly
int    numbers[] = {0, 1, 2, 3};
int    matrix[][] = {{0,1},{0,1,2}};
```

```
// a method returning an array of ints
int [] returnArray() { return new int[10]; }

// alternative declaration syntax for the method
int returnArray() [] { return new int[10]; }
```

Expressions

Java has a similar expression syntax to C. For example, the following are all valid Java expressions:

```
4+5
(4+5)*i
(i > 0) && (i < 4)
i<<1
(i > 0) ? true : false
```

In contrast to C and C++, Java doesn't, in general, have the comma operator to create compound expressions. The comma operator, however, is allowed in the initialization and continuation section of for loops. For example, the following code shows a legal use of the comma operator:

```
for (i=0,j=0; i<10 && j<20; i++,j++) {
   /* body of for loop */
}
```

Control-Flow Statements

Java has the usual set of control-flow statements found in C or C++. There are a few differences, which we'll point out.

Java has an if-then-else statement, as you might expect. The main difference between it and C is that in Java the expression in the test must return a boolean value. Zero can't be used to mean false in Java or non-zero to mean true.

```
if (boolean) {
   /* ... */
} else if (boolean) {
   /* ... */
} else {
   /* ... */
}
```

The while and do-while loops in Java are identical to C:

```
while (boolean) {
  /* ... */
}

do {
  /* ... */
} while (boolean);
```

The for loop is similar to C, with the exception that you can declare a variable in the initialization section:

```
for (expression; booleanExpression; expression) {
  /* ... */
}
```

Here's an example of declaring a variable in the for loop:

```
for (int i = 0; i < 10; i++) {
  /* ... */
}
```

In contrast to C++, the scope of the declared variables encompasses only the body of the for loop and does not extend beyond it. Thus, it is an error in the example above to reference the variable i after the for loop.

The switch statement syntax is identical to C:

```
switch (expression) {
  case Constant1:
  /* ... */
  break;
  case Constant2:
  /* ... */
  break;
  default:
  /* ... */
  break;
}
```

In addition, Java has two control-flow statements, break and continue, which take an optional label. Without the label they have the same meaning as in C.

However, if the label is supplied, the computation will continue with the statement that is labeled. For example, below is a nested for loop that makes use of the labeled continue statement:

```
outer: // label
for (int j=0; j<10; j++) {
  /* continue goes to here */
  for (int i=0; i<20; i++) {
    if (i==15) {
      continue outer; // go to the outer loop
    }
  }
}
```

Labeled break statements are particularly useful when combining a switch statement inside a for loop since the break statement has special meaning in the switch construct. Adding a label allows you to break out of a switch statement in a loop.

```
loopStart:
for (int j=0; j<10;j++) {
  /* break goes here */
  switch (j) {
    case 4:
    break;
    default:
    if ((j%2) == 0)
      break loopStart; // goes to the loop
    break;
  }
}
```

Classes and Interfaces

Java has syntax to define interfaces and classes that are templates for creating new object instances. The syntax is different than the C++ syntax for defining classes; C++ doesn't have explicit syntax for defining interfaces. The concept of interfaces and classes will be explained later in the chapter.

```
[public] interface interfaceName
    [extends   Interface1, Interface2, ...] {
  /* list of methods or static fields */
}
```

```
[ClassModifiers] class className [extends superClass]
                  [implements interfaces] {
    /* list of methods or fields */
}
```

ClassModifiers can be a combination of the following classes:

abstract   Contains abstract methods (methods without an implementa-
                tion), or it is otherwise not directly implemented.

final   Cannot be a subclass.

public   May be used by code that is outside of the class package. Only
                one public class is allowed per file, and the file must be named
                <ClassName>.java.

private   Can only be used within a file.

<empty>   If no access specifier such as public or private is given, this class
                is accessible within the current class package.

synchronizable To synchronize a statement, instances of this class can be made
                the arguments.

Methods and Fields

The syntax for defining a method in Java is similar to defining a function in C:

```
MethodModifiers ReturnType Name(argType1 arg1, ...) {
    /* body of the method */
}
```

MethodModifiers can be one of the following methods:

public   This method is accessible by methods outside of its class.

protected   This method is only accessible by a subclass.

private   This method is only accessible to other methods in this class.

<blank>   This method is accessible by methods in classes that are in the
                same package.

final   This method cannot be overridden.

static   This method is shared by all instances of this class and is in-
                voked with <Class>.method.

synchronized   This method will lock the object on entry and unlock it on exit. If the object was already locked, the method waits until the lock is released before executing.

native   This method is implemented by a stub written in another language (usually C).

The syntax for defining a field is similar to defining a structure field or a variable declaration in C:

```
FieldModifiers ReturnType FieldName;
```

In this instance, FieldModifiers operates the same as MethodModifiers, without synchronized or final methods.

Exceptions

Java has an exception mechanism that serves as a general-purpose error-handling mechanism. Exceptions will be discussed in more detail later in the chapter. There are two parts to the syntax for exception mechanism: signaling an exception and setting up an exception handler.

To signal an exception, a method simply uses the throw statement with an instance of an exception object:

```
throw new SomeException();
```

To set up an exception handler, a method uses the try-catch clause. This clause is composed of a try block, which is the code that is executed assuming no exception occurs, and a catch block, which is executed if an exception is raised.

```
try {
  /* try block */
} catch (ExceptionType e1) {
  /* catch statement 1 */
} catch (ExceptionType e2) {
  /* catch statement 2 */
}
```

There can be more than one catch block. If there is, the catch that most closely matches the class of the exception that was thrown is the one that is used. It is legal to throw the exception again inside a catch block.

Java also has an additional (and optional) clause that can be used in combination with a `try` block. It is called a `finally` clause, and it contains statements that will be executed whether or not the code terminates normally. Listing 5.2 shows how one could express that a file should be closed no matter how the code in the `try` block terminates:

LISTING 5.2 Closing a file

```
1:  File file;
2:  try {
3:      file = new File("someFile");
4:
5:      file.write("foo");
6:      file.write("bar");
7:  } catch (IOException e) {
8:      /* one of the writes failed or perhaps the file
9:         couldn't be opened. */
10:     return; // but the finally clause gets executed before
11: } finally {
12:     file.close();
13: }
```

In this case, the file.close() statement will be executed even if an exception was raised.

Other Syntax

There are statements and keywords that haven't been described in this section. Some of these will be explained later in the chapter and others can be found in the Java language spec.

 http://www.javasoft.com/hooked/language-ref.html

OBJECTS AND CLASSES

DEFINITION

An **object** is a programming abstraction that groups data with the code that operates on the data. A **class** is a template for a set of object instances.

Java is an object-oriented language, which means that programs written in Java use the programming abstraction of objects. At their most basic level, however, objects are a programming construct that packages data with the code that operates on this data. Objects are usually characterized by their class, which can be thought of as a template. Let's illustrate this by defining a class called `Rectangle` that one might use in a graphics program (see Listing 5.3).

LISTING 5.3 **Defining a class**

```
1:  /* FILE: Rectangle.java */
2:  class Rectangle {
3:      private int x;
4:      private int y;
5:      private int width;
6:      private int height;
7:
8:      public Rectangle(int x, int y, int width, int height){
9:          this.x = x;
10:         this.y = y;
11:         this.width = width;
12:         this.height = height;
13:     }
14:     public void draw() {
15:         System.out.println("Rectangle: "+ x      + "," + y +
16:                         "," + width+","+height);
17:     }
18:     public static void main(String args[]) {
19:         Rectangle r = new Rectangle(5,5,100,200);
20:         Rectangle r2 = new Rectangle(0, 10, 340, 250);
21:
22:         r.draw();
23:         r2.draw();
24:     }
25: }
```

After compiling this example with javac, we run it by executing java Rectangle. We get the following output:

```
Rectangle: 5,5,100,200
Rectangle: 0,10,340,250
```

Looking at Listing 5.3, we see that a class consists of a declaration of the class, as shown in line 1, and a set of data *fields* and *methods*. Fields are the data part of an object and are also sometimes referred to as the *state* of an object. Methods are the analogous concept for functions in an object-oriented language. They differ from functions in that they have exclusive access to the state of the object, because the object's fields are in the same scope as its methods. Access to the state can be granted to other objects as desired by the designer of the class. This access is defined by the access specifier keyword, which can used in front of data fields or methods. For example, the data fields in lines 3–6 of Listing 5.3 are all declared to be private. This declaration means that only the methods in this class are allowed to access the data.

Protecting the data in an object is an important programming tool. The fewer assumptions that are made about implementation, the more freedom the programmer has to change it. For example, we may want to change how the Rectangle class is represented at some later date (perhaps we want to rename the fields in the class or change their types). If code that uses the Rectangle class can't access the fields directly, the Rectangle class can be changed without having to change the code. This has obvious advantages for any program, but it is especially useful for large programs.

In line 8 of Listing 5.3, a method has the same name as the class. This is a special method called a *constructor*, which is responsible for initializing the object before other code can use it. This useful and important feature guarantees that an object cannot be used until its state has been properly initialized. In languages such as C, there is no good method, other than convention, to guarantee that a data structure is initialized before it is used. Using data that isn't initialized is a good source of perplexing and time-consuming bugs.

In lines 9–10 of Listing 5.3, the fields in the object are accessed as this.x and this.y. The variable this is implicitly defined inside every object's method to refer to the object itself. This variable can be used to pass the object to another method or, as in Listing 5.3, to explicitly refer to the fields in the object. The constructor uses arguments that have the same name as the fields in the object. By using the variable this, the constructor can distinguish which x and y are being assigned to the object. We can also use the this variable to call another constructor explicitly from a constructor of the class. For example, suppose we wanted to create another constructor for the Rectangle class that initialized the width and height of the rectangle to 100. We could just copy the code for the existing constructor. Or we can reuse the code for the constructor by calling it explicitly:

```
/* Constructor defaults to width,height of 100 */
public Rectangle(int x, int y) {
    /* call the other constructor with the defaults */
    this(x, y, 100, 100);
}
```

You might be wondering how you can have another method of the same name (in this case the constructor's name) in the same class. This situation is allowed as long as the constructors have different sets of arguments. In fact, any object can have methods with the same name as long as each method has different arguments. This feature, called *overloading*, is useful to express the fact that a set of methods may do the same thing conceptually, but they require different information. For example, we've defined a draw method for Rectangle that has no arguments and prints out a string to the screen with the

DEFINITION

A **constructor** is a method in a class that initializes an object before it's used.

DEFINITION

The special variable **this** can be used inside a method to refer to the object instance.

DEFINITION

Method **overloading** allows you to use the same method name with different arguments to group together related methods.

properties of Rectangle. Suppose, however, that we want to draw a rectangle graphically. To do this, we'll use a class called Graphics that can draw images on screen (in the next chapter we'll find out more about this class in the Java runtime). We can then add another draw method, which uses this Graphics class:

```
public void draw(Graphics g) {
    g.drawRect(x, y, width, height);
}
```

Now we can invoke both versions of the draw method:

```
// print out string to the screen
rect.draw();
// draw the rectangle graphically
Graphics g;
rect.draw(g);
```

Let's look at Listing 5.3 again to see how the Rectangle class is used in a program. In lines 19–20, we allocate two Rectangle objects. Objects are allocated by using the new operator in Java. This operator is somewhat like the malloc library call in C, with some important differences in Java:

▶ The new operator knows what type it needs to return, so you don't need to cast the return value.

▶ Objects are freed automatically when they're no longer needed, so there is no corresponding operator to free objects. This feature, known as *garbage collection*, frees the programmer from having to worry about memory management, which is a notoriously difficult part of writing programs (and therefore one that is often done poorly or not at all).

▶ The argument to new is the name of a constructor (possibly with some arguments) rather than just a size.

In lines 20–23 of Listing 5.3, we invoke the draw method on each new object. The syntax for invoking a method is a combination of accessing a structure and invoking a function. Because a method is tied to a specific object instance, there has to be a way to tell the method on which object instance it's operating. This is done as follows:

```
<Object>.<method>(arguments);
```

In Listing 5.3, we added the keyword static to the declaration in line 18. This keyword is used to specify that a field or method in a class is to be shared by all instances of that class. In other words, this field or method will not change regardless of which instance is used, a feature that can be useful when defining constants. It's also useful to have static methods, when it's not convenient to allocate a specific instance on which to invoke the method. The main method, in particular, must be declared this way, because there is no object instance on which it can be invoked. The syntax to invoke the static method is to use the class in the method invocation where the instance normally goes, because there is no instance that is relevant.

```
<Class>.<method>(arguments);
```

You may noticed that in Listing 5.3 there are no header files, which would be present in a program written in C or C++. This lack eliminates the need to keep a header file in sync with the implementation. In order to avoid using header files, Java replaces the include directive found in C or C++ with another statement called import that is order-independent. The need for forward declarations is eliminated, and you don't have to worry about including a file twice. The argument used by the import statement is the name of a class or a package, which is a construct that will be discussed later in this chapter.

CLASS INHERITANCE

DEFINITION

Subclassing is akin to adding a new type, except that Java remembers the relation between the types and arranges for the subclass to inherit fields and methods from the parent class.

Another useful feature in object-oriented languages is allowing classes to be related to each other through inheritance. Thus a class can be declared to be a subclass of another class. The subclass does all of the things its parent class does, plus some additional features unique to the subclass. For example, suppose we wanted to add a class that represents a circle for a graphics program that draws shapes. The program will put up a window, go through a list of shapes in a drawing, and draw each shape.

One way we could write this program is to create a class for each shape. However, the part of the graphics program that draws each shape would have to figure out what kind of shape it is drawing and invoke the right method. It might add a field to each shape to tell it what type it is and then key off this field to do the drawing, as in Listing 5.4.

LISTING 5.4 A graphics program

```
1:  switch (shapeType) {
2:  case RECTANGLE_TYPE:
3:      rectangleDraw();
4:      break;
5:  case CIRCLE_TYPE:
6:      circleDraw();
7:      break;
8:  default:
9:      ???
10: }
```

FIGURE 5.1   Inheritance hierarchy for the Shape subclasses

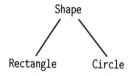

Listing 5.4 has lots of problems. When you add a new shape to the system, you must make sure all the switch statements are updated, which can be an error-prone process. Allocating a constant for the type tag is another chance to introduce errors.

A better way is to use inheritance. We'll create a class called Shape that contains the essential fields and methods that the graphics program might need. The Rectangle and Circle classes can be declared as subclasses of the Shape class. Once we do this, the graphics program will have a list of Shape objects and invoke the draw method of each shape to draw it on the screen. The graphics program doesn't have to know how the shape is represented internally or how to draw it on the screen. This is left up to the object to decide. The beauty of this scheme is that we can add as many shapes as we like to the hierarchy. In fact, the same graphics program can handle shapes it didn't know about when it was written, as long as the new shapes are subclasses of the Shape class. Figure 5.1 shows what the class hierarchy looks like when we add the Circle class.

The class hierarchy can be extended indefinitely without having the source code for the parent classes. This allows you to write a set of classes that can be extended by other people to add functionality. Much of the Java runtime is structured as a set of classes to which you can add subclasses to add functionality. Listing 5.5 shows the new version of the graphics program.

LISTING 5.5   New version of the graphics program

```
 1:  /* FILE: GraphicsProgram.java */
 2:  import java.awt.*;
 3:
 4:  class Shape {
 5:     protected Color     color;
 6:     protected int x;
 7:     protected int y;
 8:     protected Shape(Color c, int x, int y) {
 9:        color = c;
10:        this.x = x;
11:        this.y = y;
12:     }
```

```
13:    public abstract void draw();
14: }
15: class Rectangle extends Shape {
16:    private int width;
17:    private int height;
18:    public Rectangle(Color c,int x,int y,
19:                  int width,int height) {
20:      super(c, x, y);
21:      this.width = width;
22:      this.height = height;
23:    }
24:    public void draw() {
25:      System.out.println("Rectangle: "+ x      + "," + y +
26:                  "," + width+","+height);
27:    }
28: }
29: class Circle extends Shape {
30:    private int radius;
31:
32:    public Circle(Color c, int x, int y, int radius) {
33:      super(c, x, y);
34:      this.radius = radius;
35:    }
36:    public void draw() {
37:      System.out.println("Circle: "+ x + "," + y + ","
38:                  + radius);
39:    }
40: }
41: public class GraphicsProgram {
42:    public static void main(String args[]) {
43:      Shape s1 = new Rectangle(Color.red,0,5,200,300);
44:      Shape s2 = new Circle(Color.green, 20, 30, 100);
45:
46:      s1.draw();
47:      s2.draw();
48:    }
49: }
```

A key feature that lets you extend functionality for a class while being able to reuse the code in the parent class is *method overriding*. Whenever a method in a subclass has the same name and arguments as the corresponding method in the parent class, the subclass method will be the one that is used, regardless of what declared class the object has at the time of invocation. For example, in lines 42–48 in Listing 5.5, you can see that both the s1 and s2

DEFINITION

When a method in a subclass has the same name and argument signature as a method in the parent class, the method is said to **override** the parent method. It will be used in place of the parent's method.

variables are declared as instances of class Shape. Each variable, however, is initialized as a different subclass of Shape. In the case of s1, it is initialized with an instance of Rectangle, and s2 is initialized with an instance of Circle. So when s1.draw is invoked, the Rectangle's draw method is used. When s2.draw is invoked, the Circle's draw method is used. The following output is the result when we run this program:

```
Rectangle: 0,5,200,300
Circle: 20,30,100
```

Other instances of method overriding in this example are the constructors for the Rectangle and Circle classes. Constructors are a special case, however. Even though the name of the method for a constructor in a subclass isn't the same (it has to be the name of the class), the constructor is still considered to override the constructor of the parent class. One problem with method overriding is when we want to override a method to add some functionality, but we want to call the parent method to complete the method call. This is desirable because it allows us to extend functionality while reusing the code of the parent class. To do this, Java provides a special keyword called super that refers to the parent class. Thus, both the Rectangle and Circle constructors invoke the Shape constructor in lines 20 and 33 of Listing 5.5.

This same construct can be used in other methods to refer to the parent version of the method.

You might be wondering at this point how we were able to initialize s1 and s2 with instances from a subclass of Shape rather than the Shape class itself. In a traditional language such as C, you wouldn't normally be able to initialize one variable of a given type with something of a different type. To understand why it's possible to initialize variables with subclasses in an object-oriented language, we need to define how a type works in a programming language.

A *type* is basically a declaration of a set of properties associated with a given type name. These properties form a sort of contract about what a user can expect from the type. In a non-object-oriented language, a type defines its own size and what information it contains. For example, a structure definition in C implicitly defines how big the structure is, the names of the fields in the structure, and the types of each field. The contract that this type establishes is that whenever code has access to an instance of this structure, it can expect the instance to be of the same size and have the same fields as its type declaration.

In an object-oriented language, an additional clause to the contract is the set of methods that can access this type or class. In order for a language to be typesafe, it should guarantee that this contract cannot be violated by a program. Now we can explain why a subclass will do wherever its parent class would: a subclass inherits the same fields and methods as its parent class, and therefore it does not violate the contract established by the parent class.

INTERFACES

Class inheritance is helpful for reusing an implementation of a parent class, but sometimes it's overkill for a subclass to inherit the implementation. This is especially true in Java, which only allows single inheritance (in other words, only one parent class). Some languages such as C++ allow multiple inheritance. For example, suppose you have a number of classes, and you want a way to print out each class. One way is to create a parent class called `Printable` for all of the classes that have a `print` method, and each class can override this method as needed. However, since Java only has single inheritance, this approach may not be viable, because some of the classes may have parent classes that don't inherit from this `Printable` class.

The solution to this problem is to use interfaces. An interface definition is a declaration of a set of methods. It doesn't carry any implementation information so an interface cannot be implemented directly. In contrast to class inheritance, a class can implement multiple interfaces. Listing 5.6 shows an example of the `Printable` interface.

DEFINITION

An **Interface** is a declaration of a set of methods that contains no implementation code.

LISTING 5.6   The Printable interface

```
1:   interface Printable {
2:      void print();
3:   }
4:   class Cookie implements Printable {
5:      void print() {
6:         System.out.println("Cookie");
7:      }
8:   }
9:   class Cake implements Printable {
10:     void print() {
11:        System.out.println("Cake");
12:     }
13:  }
```

In this case, the Cookie and Cake classes both declare that they implement the Printable interface through the use of the `implements` keyword. You can declare that you implement more than one interface by just appending more interface names separated by commas. For example, if we want to say that the Cookie class implements another interface Edible, we would write the declaration as:

```
class Cookie implements Printable, Edible {
}
```

In a similar fashion to classes, interfaces can inherit from each other. For example, if the Printable interface also wants to include the methods from the Writable interface, it would be declared as follows:

```
interface Printable extends Writable {
    void print();
}
```

Of course, an interface can't be declared to be an implementation of another interface, because an interface cannot contain implementation code.

PACKAGES

In addition to classes that allow you to group fields and methods, Java has a construct called a *package* that allows you to group related classes. Selected classes from this package can be used by other classes not in the package through the use of the import command. Suppose that in the graphics example we would like to create a package of related shape classes that well call the shape package. We can do this by making each shape class its own file and putting the statement package shape at the beginning of each file.

```
/* FILE: Shape.java */
package shape;

... definition of the Shape class ...

/* FILE: Rectangle.java */
package shape;

... definition of the Rectangle class ...

/* FILE: Circle.java */
package shape;

... definition of the Circle class ...
```

We can then rewrite the GraphicsProgram class to use the Shape package by putting at the beginning of the file:

```
/* FILE: GraphicsProgram.java */
import shape.*;
```

Using shape.* means that all of the classes in the shape package are imported or used in this file. Note that we can also use a class in another package without the import statement by explicitly putting the name of the package before the class. For example, in the GraphicsProgram.java file we can use shape.Rectangle or shape.Circle without using the import statement. Using the import statement is a shortcut that allows you to avoid prefixing the package name in front of every class in the package.

Java comes with a number of class packages that are available for your use. These packages are:

java.lang	Contains essential Java classes. By default it is implicitly imported into every Java file, so you don't need to specify import java.lang.* at the beginning of every file.
java.io	Contains classes used to do input/output. A lot of classes serve to let you stream data in and out to different sources.
java.util	Contains utility classes such as hashtables and vectors.
java.net	Contains classes to use network connections. These can be used in combination with the classes in java.io to read/write information from the network.
java.awt	Contains classes that let you write platform-independent GUI applications.
java.applet	Contains classes that let you create Java applets that will run in any Java-compatible browser.

A huge number of classes are contained in these six packages, so describing them here in detail is beyond the scope of this book. Instead we'll describe some of the classes from these packages as we go along. The next chapter in particular will describe classes in java.applet and java.awt in more detail.

EXCEPTIONS

In languages such as C, runtime errors are handled in a variety of ways. If you try to access a null pointer, the system may either abort your program with an error message, or the system itself may freeze up (depending upon which operating system you are using). In addition, if you want to signal an error in a function, you have to use a special return value to tell the caller of the function an error occurred or use an output variable to signal the error when a return value is inappropriate. In other words, error handling is not consistent. It also leads to somewhat cumbersome code. Whenever a function has the possibility of returning an error code, it has to be checked and appropriate action has to be taken, such as in the following piece of code:

```
if (!writeToFile(stuff)) {
  /* error */
}
if (!writeToFile(more stuff)) {
  /* error */
}
```

If we want to write robust code, we have to check the return code of writeToFile each time we call it and deal with it in some manner. We also have to ensure that the error code would be propagated up the call stack if necessary. It'd be nice if we could write code with the assumption that there would be no errors, but have the code able to deal with errors if they arose, nevertheless. If error handling were uniform, there would be a greater chance that it'd be done correctly in all the classes, even ones that were written by different programmers. The way to achieve these benefits is to use Java exceptions.

Exceptions provide a clean way for a method to abort whatever it was doing and signal to the caller of the method that something went wrong. In contrast to methods of error handling that return error codes, the caller can ignore the exception that was raised and let the exception propagate up the call stack until one of the methods handles the exception. A call stack is just the sequence of method invocations. To show the value of exceptions, suppose there is a method called writeStuff that uses return error codes, as in Listing 5.7.

LISTING 5.7   Error handling using return error codes

```
 1:  void writeStuff(String stuff, String moreStuff) {
 2:    if (!writeToFile(stuff)) {
 3:      /* error */
 4:      return;
 5:    }
 6:    if (!writeToFile(moreStuff)) {
 7:      /* error */
 8:      return;
 9:    }
10:  }
```

If we rewrite Listing 5.7 using exceptions and assume that writeToFile will raise an exception, Listing 5.8 is the result.

LISTING 5.8   Error handling using exceptions

```
1:  void writeStuff(String stuff, String moreStuff) {
2:    try {
3:      writeToFile(stuff);
4:      writeToFile(moreStuff);
5:    } catch (Exception e) {
6:      e.printStackTrace();
7:      return;
8:    }
9:  }
```

Listing 5.8 uses the try-catch clause, a Java construct that was introduced earlier in this chapter. The statements inside the braces of the try block are written as if no exceptions happened. If an exception happens anywhere inside the try block, the statements in the catch block are executed. In Listing 5.8, the only thing we do is invoke the printStackTrace method on the exception, which prints out the stack trace to the screen and then return from the method.

To raise an exception, we use the throw operator in Java. The argument to this operator is an instance of a subclass of the Exception class. For example, using the throw operator with the writeToFile method in Listing 5.8 would result in Listing 5.9.

LISTING 5.9   Using the throw operator

```
1:  void writeToFile(String something) {
2:    if (fileDoesNotExist) {
3:      throw new FileNotFoundException();
4:    } else {
5:      /* write something to the file */
6:    }
7:  }
```

The throw statement in line 3 of Listing 5.9 aborts the method and raises the exception through the call stack. If there is a catch clause in the caller that matches the class of the exception or one of its parent classes, then the exception stops there and the catch clause will handle the problem. However, if the caller doesn't have a catch clause, then the exception keeps traveling down the stack until it finds a catch clause. The program is aborted if there is no catch clause. This is depicted in Figure 5.2.

FIGURE 5.2   What happens when an exception is raised

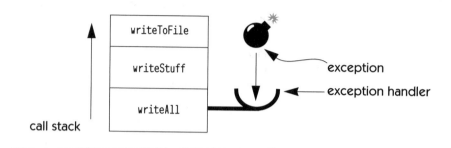

THREADS

Another major Java feature is language support for threads. A thread refers to a thread of execution in a program. Normally, programs have only a single thread of execution, and this can make some things awkward to do. For example, a GUI application is typically expected to respond to user input while it is doing background computation. To accomplish this, the application might try to interrupt the computation every so often to see if there is any user input. This is both awkward and dangerous, because the computation might be using methods that weren't written to be interrupted.

With thread support, however, this application would have two threads of control: one to process the user events in the GUI and another to do background computation. On a computer with only one processor, both threads aren't actually processing in parallel. Rather, at regular intervals or when the thread is waiting for something, the computation will switch from one thread to another. This gives the appearance of parallelism. On computers with multiple processors, there is potential for the computations to truly happen in parallel if the underlying system supports it.

Let's look at an example of a multi-threaded program in Java (see Listing 5.10). It basically is a program that creates a class called Printer. The input for this class is a string to print out, a count for how many times to print the string, and a time interval to sleep between the times the string is printed. This class creates a thread for itself, which will print the string, wait the specified amount of time, and repeat this process until it's printed the string the required number of times.

DEFINITION

A **thread** is all of the states necessary for a computation. Multiple thread support allows multiple computations to happen in parallel.

LISTING 5.10   **A multithreaded program**

```
1:  public class Printer implements Runnable {
2:      Thread printerThread;
3:      String string;
```

```
4:    int count;
5:    int sleepTime;
6:
7:    public Printer(String s, int howMany, int sleep) {
8:       count = howMany;
9:       string = s;
10:      sleepTime = sleep;
11:      printerThread = new Thread(this);
12:      printerThread.start();
13:   }
14:   public void run() {
15:      while (count -- > 0) {
16:         System.out.println(string);
17:         try {
18:            Thread.sleep(sleepTime);
19:         } catch (Exception e) {
20:            return;
21:         }
22:      }
23:   }
24:   public static void main(String args[]) {
25:      new Printer("Ping", 5, 300);
26:      new Printer("Pong", 5, 500);
27:   }
28: }
```

When you run the program in Listing 5.10, you should see the following output:

```
Ping
Pong
Ping
Pong
Ping
Ping
Pong
Ping
Pong
Pong
```

Notice that the output from each thread in Listing 5.10 is interleaved, because the Java runtime is switching between the two threads. In a single-threaded program, you would have to do this interleaving manually by coding a function that switches between the two strings at given intervals. This may not seem so daunting in a simple program such as the one in Listing 5.10, but as more activities need to be interleaved, the task of interleaving manually becomes much more difficult.

Let's look at the code from Listing 5.10 in more detail. In line 1, the Printer class is declared to implement the Runnable interface. This is an interface found in the java.lang package, and it's basically defined as:

```
package java.lang;

public interface Runnable {
   void run();
}
```

In other words, any class that implements Runnable should define a run method.

The constructor for the Thread class takes an instance of the Runnable interface and invokes the run method when the thread is started. When the run method returns, the thread will automatically exit. In Listing 5.10, the Printer threads terminate when they've finished printing the required number of strings.

Threads in Java can also have associated priorities, which means that threads with higher priority will run over threads with lower priority. Priorities are useful in certain cases when you want certain threads to execute whenever they aren't waiting on anything. In general, it's bad practice to rely on strict priorities. They should instead be viewed as hints to the system as to which threads should have access to the processor(s) before others.

MONITORS AND SYNCHRONIZATION

When there are multiple threads accessing data or invoking methods that affect the state of an object, it is necessary to protect the data from simultaneous access by multiple threads. The order in which threads run is not predictable, so if you allow multiple threads to change data simultaneously, the data may not be in a consistent state afterward. For example, suppose an object has two fields that need to be kept consistent: one is an array of numbers and the other is a count of how many numbers are in the array (see Listing 5.11).

LISTING 5.11   A program resulting in inconsistent data

```
1:  class NumberArray {
2:     int count = 0;
3:     int numbers[] = new numbers[20];
```

```
 4:     void addNumber(int n) {
 5:       numbers[count] = n;
 6:       count++;
 7:     }
 8:     void print() {
 9:       for (int i = 0; i < count; i++) {
10:         System.out.println(numbers[i]);
11:       }
12:     }
13: }
```

Imagine what would happen if one thread adds numbers to an instance of the NumberArray class, while another thread is printing out this instance. This can lead to inconsistencies. The print method might not get the latest value of the count variable, because the other thread is incrementing the value in parallel. This would lead to the print method not printing out the latest state for this instance. A more serious problem is that the number array may hold invalid entries when the program is finished executing. To see how this might happen, consider Listing 5.11, where two threads are executing the addNumber method. In this situation, the following ordering leads to an inconsistent state:

```
thread 1: numbers[count] = 12;
thread 2: numbers[count] = 13;
thread 1: count++;
thread 2: count++;
```

The result of this ordering is that the same slot in the array has been used to store two numbers, but the count was incremented twice. Therefore, the next slot in the array is also counted by the count variable although it contains an invalid value.

The solution to this problem is to use the synchronized keyword in Java. By declaring the addNumber and the print method to be synchronized methods, Java will automatically disallow one thread from invoking the synchronized method if it is already being executed by another thread. When any of the synchronized methods terminate, the threads that are waiting can then proceed to execute the desired method. Listing 5.12 is a reformulation of Listing 5.11 with the proper synchronized keywords added.

LISTING 5.12 A program with consistent data using synchronized methods

```
1:  class NumberArray {
2:    int count = 0;
3:    int numbers[] = new numbers[20];
```

```
4:    synchronized void addNumber(int n) {
5:       numbers[count] = n;
6:       count++;
7:    }
8:    synchronized void print() {
9:       for (int i = 0; i < count; i++) {
10:          System.out.println(numbers[i]);
11:       }
12:    }
13: }
```

Each object has an object called a *monitor* that is associated with it. This monitor acts as a gatekeeper for the object and will only let in one synchronized method at a time. When the synchronized method terminates, the monitor is unlocked, giving another synchronized method the chance to start executing.

Thread programming can be challenging. Because many of the problems that arise from incorrect synchronization strategies are timing-related, the problems often aren't apparent. When they do appear, they are often hard to diagnose. Most thread programming problems can be characterized as one of the following errors:

▶ An object's method is changing the state of an object, but it is being executed by multiple threads. This was the problem in Listing 5.11.

▶ Two or more synchronized methods depend upon each other, which can lead to deadlock, where two or more threads can't continue because they are waiting on each other indefinitely. For example, consider Listing 5.13.

LISTING 5.13 An example of deadlock

```
1:  class Printer implements Runnable {
2:     Input input;
3:     synchronized void print() {
4:        input.write();
5:     }
6:     synchronized void write() {
7:     }
8:     public void run() {
9:        print();
10:    }
11: }
12: class Input implements Runnable {
13:    Printer printer;
14:    synchronized void write() {
15:       printer.sendData();
16:    }
```

```
17:     public void run() {
18:        write();
19:     }
20:  }
21:  class Deadlock {
22:     public static void main(String args[]) {
23:        Printer p = new Printer();
24:        Input   i = new Input();
25:
26:        p.input = i;
27:        i.printer = p;
28:        Thread t1 = new Thread(p);
29:        Thread t2 = new Thread(i);
30:        t1.start();
31:        t2.start();
32:     }
33:  }
```

DEFINITION

Deadlock occurs when two or more threads can't continue because they are waiting on each other indefinitely.

In Listing 5.13, deadlock could occur with the execution of the threads running the Printer object and the Input object. These threads could be interleaved in such a way that the Printer object locks its monitor in preparation to execute its print method. Subsequently, the Input object locks its own monitor in preparation to execute its write method. Next, the print method wants to invoke the write method on the Input object, but the monitor for the Input object is locked, so the print method waits. Similarly, the Input object wants to grab the Printer object's monitor to execute its sendData method, but the Printer object's monitor is locked, so the Input object also waits. However, they're waiting on each other, so this situation continues indefinitely, and the two threads are stuck (see Figure 5.3).

FIGURE 5.3 A deadlock situation. Each thread is waiting for the other to unlock an object.

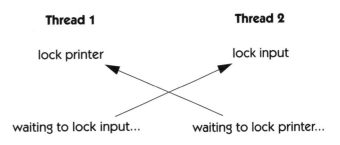

In the face of deadlock problems, there are some simple strategies that one can follow to write correctly threaded programs:

▶ Use threads to solve a specific task that needs to run in parallel with other tasks. Doing this means that a thread has a well-defined job. Having a well-defined job means it's easier to identify the places in the code where the thread needs to be synchronized. In Listing 5.13, there was no need to create two threads to execute the methods, because they depended on each other anyway.

▶ Be careful when invoking an object's synchronized method from another synchronized method. If multiple threads can execute these methods independently, this can lead to deadlock.

▶ Try to hold locks for the shortest time possible. It's not a good idea to hold a lock while doing something that might take a long time, such as doing network I/O.

PROGRAMMING WITH JAVA

This chapter introduced you to the Java language in more depth. It was not meant as an exhaustive account of the language, but as enough background to get started programming with Java. As you write more Java code, we think you'll appreciate the simplicity of the language as well as its lack of ambiguity.

6

Building an Applet

If you'd like to create applets of your own, this chapter will get you started. It'll teach you the basic skills necessary to write an applet in Java and show you the more sophisticated alternatives that are possible with the Java API. You should have some programming experience to get the most from what follows. The source code for the applets presented in this chapter is collected for you in Appendix C.

THE APPLET CLASS

In this section, we discuss the methods in the applet class and explain how to ensure that your applet is well-behaved with respect to its environment. We also examine methods that provide essential features in applets.

The Applet API

The classes in the applet API are defined simply to be all of the java.* packages, as discussed in Chapter 5 (see "Packages" on page 110). Applets built using these classes will run in any environment supporting Java.

Lifecycle Methods

The applet lifecycle is comprised of the steps an applet goes through from the time that it's loaded to the time that it's no longer accessible and is reclaimed by the system. See Figure 6.1.

FIGURE 6.1   The applet lifecycle

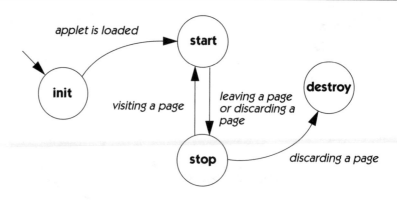

Each circle in Figure 6.1 represents a phase in the applet lifecycle. The arrows represent transitions, and the text in italics represents an action that causes the transition. Each phase in the lifecycle is marked by a method invocation to the applet, so the applet can take appropriate action. You never need to invoke these methods directly, because the runtime system will invoke them when necessary. For example, if you activated an applet inside a Web page with your Web browser, and you left that page to go to another, the browser would invoke the stop method on the applet.

The lifecycle methods in an applet, and their purpose, follow:

void init()   Called once after an applet has been loaded into the system. This is a good place to do any necessary initialization.

void start()   Called to inform the applet that it should take any action to start running. For example, applets that use threads for animation would start the threads. This method is called after init and whenever the applet is revisited in a Web page.

void stop()   Called to inform the applet that it should stop its execution. For an applet that uses threads, this method should be used to stop the threads. Typically it's called when the Web page that contains this applet is replaced by another page.

void destroy() Called to tell the applet that it's being reclaimed from the system and that it should destroy any resources it has allocated. An applet that uses threads would destroy them in this method. Note that stop will always be called before destroy.

It's not required that every applet override these methods. In fact, the simple applet introduced in the previous chapter overrides the paint method because it doesn't need to take any special action for any of the lifecycle methods. However, if your applet uses threads or allocates any resources that need to be freed, it has to override the appropriate lifecycle methods in order to be a well-behaved applet.

HTML Tag Methods

The following methods are used to find out information about an applet, such as the URL of the document in which it's embedded or the parameters that were passed to the applet through the HTML tag.

URL getDocumentBase()

> Returns the URL of the document that contains the applet. The URL class returned is in the java.net package, and it has many methods that allow you to manipulate and read the contents of the URL. This class is described in a little more detail below.

URL getCodeBase()

> Returns the URL of the applet itself, which may differ from the URL of the document it's in.

String getParameter (String name)

> Returns the value of a named parameter in the HTML tag. For example, an applet tag is specified as:

```
<applet code="Fun.class" width=50 height=50>
<param name=Color value="red">
</applet>
```

> Calling getParameter("Color") for the above applet will return the value "red." If the parameter wasn't specified in the HTML tag, then this method returns null.

The URL class in java.net lets you specify a URL programmatically and also retrieve the contents to which the URL points. There are many methods that comprise the URL class, which we won't go into here. For the purposes of this chapter, we'll just describe some common ways of allocating URL objects.

The simplest way to specify a URL is to initialize it while passing in a string:

```
URL someURL = new URL("http://www.javasoft.com/");
```

This creates an absolute URL, because it's fully specified in the string. For many of the applet methods, it's desirable to specify an URL that is relative to the URL of the applet. To do this, we simply use a different constructor that takes a URL as an argument and a URL specification that is relative to the given URL. For example, if we wanted to form a URL that points to images/Smiley.gif, we'd do the following:

```
URL   documentURL = new URL("http://www.javasoft.com/");
URL   imageURL = new URL(documentURL, "images/Smiley.gif");
```

If we want to print out the result to the screen (useful for debugging), we can do the following:

```
System.out.println(imageURL);
```

This would print out:

```
http://www.javasoft.com/images/Smiley.gif
```

Media Support

The applet class includes methods for getting images and sounds from URLs, which makes it easy to use these media types in your applets. In the case of images, format conversion from GIF or JPEG is done automatically for you, and you'll even see incremental image rendering while the image data is being loaded over the network.

Image getImage(URL url)

> Returns an image object that can be painted on the screen. The URL that is given as an argument should be an absolute URL. Note that this method will return immediately whether or not the image exists. When an attempt to draw the image is made, the data will load. The graphics primitives that draw images will incrementally paint an image on the screen.

Image getImage(URL url, String name)

> Gets an image when it's given a URL and a URL specifier that's relative to it.

AudioClip getAudioClip(URL url)

> Gets the audio data that the given URL points to and returns an object of type AudioClip, which allows you to play the sound clip. This object is described below.

AudioClip getAudioClip(URL url, String name)

> Gets an audio clip if it's given a URL and a URL specifier that's relative to it.

void play(URL url)
>Plays an audio clip directly if it's given an absolute URL.

void play(URL url, String name)
>Plays an audio clip directly given a URL and a URL specifier that's relative to it.

The AudioClip class is a very simple abstraction that lets you play a sound clip. Multiple AudioClip objects can be playing at the same time, and the sound will be mixed together to produce a composite. It has only three methods.

void play()   Start playing the sound clip.

void loop()   Play this sound clip in a loop.

void stop()   Stop playing this sound clip.

Manipulating the Applet's Environment

Some applets want to affect the environment in which they're running. For example, if an applet is running inside a Web browser, it may want to replace the Web page that the browser is viewing. The applet API has limited support for this feature, because it can't be assumed that an applet is running in a Web browser. Even if the applet is running in a Java-compatible Web browser, the browser may have such different features from others that a unified interface may not be feasible. You need to use the methods in the AppletContext class to get around this necessary limitation of the applet API.

AppletContext getAppletContext()
>Returns an instance of the AppletContext class, which allows the applet to affect its environment in limited ways.

Applet getApplet(String name)
>Returns an applet if it's been given the applet's name. The name can be set in the HTML tag by setting the name attribute. If an applet with this name doesn't exist in the current page, then this method returns null.

Enumeration getApplets()
>Returns all the applets on the current page (subject to security considerations).

void showDocument(URL url)
>Replaces the Web page currently viewed with the given URL. This method may be ignored if the application accessing the applet isn't a Web browser.

Applet Information

Some applet methods are designed to communicate information about your applet or show messages on the screen concerning it.

void showStatus(String status)

Prints out a status string to the screen.

String getAppletInfo()

When overridden, returns informative string about the applet such as its author, copyright, or version.

String[][] getParameterInfo()

When overridden, returns an array that describes the parameters that this applet knows how process. This kind of information would be useful for learning what parameters are applicable to this applet, or it could be used in the future by authoring environments to allow you to configure an applet graphically. Each element in the array is an array of three strings that have the following form:

{*name, type, comment*}

Below is an example of how to define this method for an applet that allows one parameter, Color, which is the color the applet will use to draw.

```
public String[][] getParameterInfo() {
        String info[][] = {{"Color",
                                "String",
                            "foreground color"}};
        return info;
}
```

Security Considerations

Applets are executable content that run inside an application, such as a Web browser. This executable content can be fetched from the network, which means that code that is possibly untrusted runs inside the application. Java and the applet API have many security safeguards that minimize the risk of running applets, but these safeguards mean that applet programmers will be limited in what they can do.

The security model for Java applets treats the applets as untrusted code running inside a trusted environment. For example, when you install a copy of a Web browser on your machine, you're trusting it to be code-suitable to run in your environment. Typically, users are (or should be) careful about installing programs on their machines, especially if the programs came from somewhere on the network. An applet, on the other hand, is loaded from the network without any assumptions as to its trustworthiness.

The Java language and the applet runtime are written to guard against untrusted applets. These safeguards are implemented by verifying that the bytecodes for the applet's classes don't break the basic rules of the language and the access restrictions inside the runtime. Only when these constraints have been satisfied is the applet code allowed to execute. When it does execute, it's tagged as being an applet inside the Java interpreter. This tag allows the runtime classes to determine whether a piece of code should be allowed to invoke a certain method. For example, an applet is restricted in the set of hosts to which it can open a network connection or in the set of URLs it can access. Together these sets of restrictions constitute a security policy. In the future, Java will have a richer set of policies, including ones that use encryption and authentication to allow applets to have more capabilities.

The current security policy affects the features an applet can use. This is a summary of the policy as it's defined as of the writing of this book:

▶ Applets will likely be restricted in the file access they can do. In particular, writing files and perhaps even reading files won't be a standard feature that can be relied on in all browsers supporting Java applets.

▶ Network connections will be restricted to only connecting to the host from which the applet comes. For URLs, only those that point to the applet's host can be opened.

▶ An applet won't be able to use any methods that would result in running arbitrary, unchecked code on its behalf. This includes methods that run arbitrary programs as well as the method that loads dynamic libraries.

Although this set of restrictions rules out some interesting applets, establishing security for executable content is important. We anticipate, however, that future security models will allow authenticated applets to do away with these restrictions.

THE ABSTRACT WINDOW TOOLKIT

This section is a brief overview of the window toolkit included with the standard applet runtime. Once you know the basics of the window toolkit described in this chapter, it should be easier to learn the other features in the toolkit, which aren't described here.

The Abstract Window Toolkit (AWT) is a GUI toolkit designed to work across multiple platforms. As such, it doesn't include all of the features of a particular platform, but it has a common set of features that can be supported on most platforms. To cope with the need for additional features, the AWT is designed to be extensible, so you can make your own GUI controls in Java and be assured they will run on all the platforms. Figure 6.2 shows the class hierarchy for the main AWT classes.

There are other important classes that aren't shown in Figure 6.2, but they'll be introduced later. For the moment, let's explain the purpose of each of the classes above.

Component
: The parent class of many of the AWT classes. Its basic purpose is to represent something that has a position and a size and can be painted on the screen as well as receive input events.

Container
: The parent class of all components and one that can contain other classes. Container has a useful helper object called a LayoutManager, which is a class that positions the components inside the container according to some policy. There are a few sample layouts included with the AWT, but you can also write your own if the ones that come with the toolkit aren't adequate for your use.

Window
: A top-level window that has no border.

Frame
: A top-level window that has a border and can also have an associated MenuBar object. The MenuBar class will be explained in more detail later.

Dialog
: A top-level window used to create dialogs. It has the ability to be modal, which means that only this window will receive input from the user.

FileDialog
: A dialog that uses the native file chooser dialog to select a file from the file system.

Panel
: A subclass of Container that can be used inside other containers, allowing you to make more intricate layouts by combining them with subpanels, or subclassed to create custom containers.

FIGURE 6.2   Class hierarchy for the main AWT classes

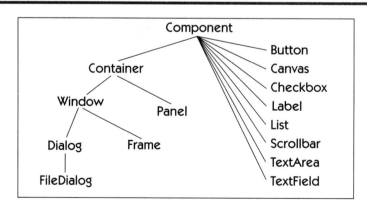

Button   A GUI button for which you can define an action that will happen when the button is pressed.

Canvas   A general-purpose component that lets you paint or trap input events from the user. It can be used to create graphics, or it can be used as a base class that can be subclassed in order to create your own custom components.

Checkbox   A component that has an "on" or "off" state. You can attach actions to it that will be triggered when the state changes.

Label   A component that displays a string at a certain location.

List   A scrolling list of strings.

Scrollbar   A scrollbar that can be used to build scrollable canvases.

TextArea   A simple text-editing component.

TextField   A single-line text component that can be used to build forms.

The scope of this book won't permit us to describe in detail all of the features of the AWT. However, we will cover a few basic points about how it has been designed to be used. Because the AWT is a simple GUI toolkit in comparison to others, these few points should allow you to get started. We'll begin by presenting some of the fundamental classes you need to understand to use the AWT.

Event

Whenever there is an event that a component needs to process, the AWT delivers it to the component. The Event class has information that describes the event. If the component doesn't handle the event, the event will be forwarded to the container that contains the component. This enables a container to handle all the events that its children don't wish to handle.

Component

The Component class can be thought of as a visible UI object that responds to user input and paints itself on the screen. Among the methods that appear in the Component class are:

Dimension size()

Returns the width and height of the component as a Dimension object, which has width and height fields.

Rectangle bounds()

Returns the coordinates of this component. The Rectangle class has x, y, width, and height fields.

```
void enable()
```
> Makes the component sensitive to user input. This is the default.

```
void disable()
```
> Makes the component insensitive to user input.

```
void show()
```
> Shows the component.

```
void paint(Graphics g)
```
> Called by the AWT when it thinks the component needs to be repainted.

```
void repaint()
```
> Used to request that the AWT repaint the component.

```
void update(Graphics g)
```
> Called by the AWT when it has invoked the repaint method. It defaults to calling paint.

```
boolean mouseEnter(Event e, int x, int y)
```
> Called when the mouse enters the bounds of this component. It should return false if the event needs to continue propagating up the containment hierarchy. Otherwise it returns true.

```
boolean mouseExit(Event e, int x, int y)
```
> Called when the mouse leaves the bounds of the component.

```
boolean mouseMove(Event e, int x, int y)
```
> Called when the mouse moves inside the component without any buttons pressed.

```
boolean mouseDrag(Event e, int x, int y)
```
> Called when the mouse moves inside the component with a button pressed.

```
boolean keyDown(Event e, int key)
```
> Called when a key has been pressed on the component.

```
boolean handleEvent(Event e)
```
> Traps any event to the component. By default this method looks at the event and calls one of the above methods. If you override this method, you should return the result of calling its superclass version.

```
Dimension preferredSize()
```
> Returns the dimension that this component would like to be.

```
Dimension minimumSize()
```
> Returns the minimum size that this component can be.

Container

The Container class is a subclass of the Component class. Container knows how to display embedded components (which can themselves be instances of the Container class). Among the methods in this class are:

void add(Component c)
> Adds a component to the container.

void add(String name, Component c)
> Adds the component and associates the given name with this component. Some layout managers use this name to make layout decisions.

void setLayout(LayoutManager l)
> Sets the layout manager for this component. This is an object that's responsible for positioning the components inside the container. The advantage of doing this rather than explicitly positioning the components is that this solution works in a multiplatform environment and also the layout manager knows what to do when the container is resized.

Graphics

This object contains many methods for rendering graphics. For example, it has methods to draw strings, shapes, and images on the screen. Some of its methods will be demonstrated in this chapter. The others can be learned by just trying them out in your applets.

Listing 6.1 shows an example program that only creates a button on screen. We'll explain the details of how it works later on.

LISTING 6.1 Button example program

```
 1:  /* File: ButtonExample.java */
 2:  import java.awt.*;
 3:  public class ButtonExample extends Frame {
 4:     public ButtonExample() {
 5:        setTitle("ButtonExample");
 6:        setLayout(new FlowLayout());
 7:        add(new Button("Push Me"));
 8:        pack();
 9:        show();
10:     }
11:     public boolean action(Event e, Object arg) {
12:        System.out.println(((Button)e.target).getLabel());
13:     }
```

```
14:    public static void main(String args[]) {
15:      new ButtonExample();
16:    }
17: }
```

You can compile this program with the following command:

```
javac ButtonExample.java
```

Once it's compiled, you can run the program by doing the following:

```
java ButtonExample
```

This should cause a window to appear on your screen that looks roughly like Figure 6.3 (it may vary depending on whether you're using a PC or a Solaris machine).

Now let's go through the lines in Listing 6.1 and explain how it works. Line 5 sets the title of the frame to the string "ButtonExample." Another way to do this is to invoke the frame constructor that takes a title as an argument:

```
super("ButtonExample");
```

In line 6, we set the layout manager for this frame. This object is responsible for laying out the components inside the frame when the frame size changes (try resizing the frame with the example and notice how the button stays centered in the frame).

Line 7 adds the new button to the frame. The Button constructor takes an argument, which is the label of the button.

Line 8 calculates how big the frame has to be in order for the contents to fit and resizes the frame to that size.

Up to now, the frame wasn't visible. Line 9 makes the frame visible.

The action method defined above is called when any of the components in the frame have been activated. In the case of the button, this happens when it's pressed. This example prints out the label of the button when the button is pressed.

FIGURE 6.3   Creating a button on screen

Now we're ready to start writing some applets. More of the API to the AWT will be demonstrated in the rest of the chapter, as well as useful techniques for making configurable applets that do graphics, animation, and use the AWT components to provide a user interface to your applets.

SIMPLE GRAPHICS

We begin our project with an applet that simply draws a line. We'll call it GraphicsApplet. Listing 6.2 shows the entire definition for this applet.

LISTING 6.2 Drawing a line with GraphicsApplet

```
1:  /* File: GraphicsApplet.java */
2:  import java.awt.*;
3:  import java.applet.*;
4:
5:  public class GraphicsApplet extends Applet {
6:     public void paint(Graphics g) {
7:        Dimension r = size();
8:        g.setColor(Color.red);
9:        g.drawLine(0, 0, r.width, r.height);
10:    }
11: }
```

To run the applet, we can embed the applet tag in a Web page, such as the following:

```
<title>GraphicsApplet</title>
<applet code="GraphicsApplet.class" width=200 height=200>
</applet>
```

Running this Web page in a Java-compatible browser or the Appletviewer program produces the applet shown in Figure 6.4.

Now let's go through a line-by-line account of how this all works.

Lines 2 and 3 in Listing 6.2 declare the necessary import statements so that all of the classes that are needed in this program are known by the Java interpreter. This is similar to include statements in C except you don't have to worry about including things only once or by ordering problems.

In line 5 of Listing 6.2, we declare GraphicsApplet to be a subclass of Applet. Most of the methods inherited from Applet have an acceptable default action. The only method we override is the paint method in line 6. This method will be called whenever the applet needs to have the screen repainted. This will happen when the applet is shown for the first time, when a page containing the applet is revisited, or whenever the window system decides that the

FIGURE 6.4   Running the GraphicsApplet

applet needs to be redisplayed, such as when a window that was obscuring the applet is removed. The paint method is passed to a Graphics object, which has many useful methods for drawing things on the screen.

In line 7, we find out how big the applet is on the screen by calling the bounds method. This returns to us an object of type Rectangle, which has the following fields:

x   the x coordinate of this rectangle

y   the y coordinate of this rectangle

width   the width of the rectangle

height   the height of the rectangle

As in most graphics systems, the coordinate system for applets defines y values increasing from top to bottom and x values increasing from left to right, with the origin at the top-left corner. See Figure 6.5.

In line 8 of Listing 6.2, we use the setColor method in Graphics to set the foreground color to red. We use one of the predefined colors in the Color class to do this. The Color class is a class that represents colors in what is known as "rgb" format. This format represents a color as a mixture of red, green, and blue components. Each component can be a value from 0 to 255. In addition, the Color class has static constants that represent well-known colors such red, green, blue, cyan, magenta, yellow, and so on.

Finally, in line 9 we get to do some drawing. In this case, we just draw a line from the top-left corner of the applet, which is at (0,0) to the bottom-right corner, which we find from the Dimension object that was returned by the size method. Note that the applet can paint as if its top-left corner is at (0,0) even though physically the top-left corner might appear in some other coor-

FIGURE 6.5 Coordinate system for applets

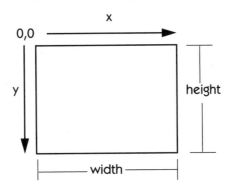

dinate on the page. This simplifies the graphics operations for the programmer.

Let's look at a slight variation in this program: we'll use another of the graphics primitives to draw a rectangle instead of a line. To do this, we change line 9 to:

```
g.drawRect(10, 10, r.width - 20, r.height - 20);
```

We subtract 20 from both the width and the height, because the drawRect primitive is defined to draw on the outside border of the given rectangle. In this case, we want the rectangle to be on the inside of the applet's boundaries. Running this example will give you the result in Figure 6.6.

FIGURE 6.6 Drawing a rectangle

DRAWING STRINGS

Now let's do something a bit more complicated. We'd like to change the applet so it displays a string in the center of the applet. To do this, we need to use the drawString graphics primitive. Since we want the string to be centered, we also need to use the font APIs to figure out how wide the string will be when printed on the screen. First, we'll add a field to GraphicsApplet to hold the font we're using:

```
public class GraphicsApplet extends Applet {
    Font appFont;
```

Now we add the init method, which is inherited from the Applet class. It's called when the applet is first loaded into a browser, so you have a chance to do any one-time initializations you need:

```
public void init() {
    appFont = new Font("Helvetica",Font.BOLD,14);
}
```

Now we'll define a method to draw a string centered in the middle of the applet. In order to center the string, we need to subtract the width of the string we're drawing from the applet's width. We divide that by two, and that gives us the x-coordinate. We do a similar process to arrive at the y-coordinate, this time using the height of the font we're using rather than the width of the string. See Listing 6.3.

LISTING 6.3   Drawing a centered string

```
 1:    public void drawCenteredString(String s,
 2:                        Color color,
 3:                            Graphics g,
 4:                        Dimension r) {
 5:      FontMetrics fm = g.getFontMetrics();
 6:      int sWidth = fm.stringWidth(s);
 7:      int sHeight = fm.getHeight();
 8:      g.setColor(color);
 9:      g.drawString(s,(r.width - sWidth)/2,
10:              (r.height - sHeight)/2);
11:    }
```

In line 5 is the FontMetrics object for the Graphics object that was passed in. The FontMetrics object has useful information about the current font. The par-

FIGURE **6.7**   Applet that draws a centered string

ticular FontMetrics methods we're interested in here are stringWidth, which calculates how wide a string will be in the current font, and getHeight, which returns the height of the current font. These values are then used in line 9 to draw the string centered in the applet as described above. Note that drawCenteredString calls getFontMetrics each time, because its result should not be cached. The reason for this is that a different kind of Graphics object may be passed in to the paint method (for example, a printing graphics object), so the result of getFontMetrics might be different. Listing 6.4 shows what the new paint method looks like.

LISTING **6.4   The new paint method**

```
1:    public void paint(Graphics g) {
2:        Dimension r = size();
3:        g.setFont(appFont);
4:        drawCenteredString("Graphics",Color.red,g,r);
5:    }
6:  }
```

Figure 6.7 shows what the new applet should look like.

DRAWING IMAGES

Now let's use the Graphics primitive drawImage to draw an image. We'll use a version of the drawImage method that scales the image you want to draw so that the image will fill the bounds of the applet. See Listing 6.5.

LISTING 6.5 Drawing an Image

```
1:  import java.awt.*;
2:  import java.applet.*;
3:
4:  public class GraphicsApplet extends Applet {
5:     Image image;
6:     public void init() {
7:        image = getImage(getDocumentBase(),
8:                         "images/cupHJbelow.gif");
9:     }
10:    public void paint(Graphics g) {
11:       Rectangle r = bounds();
12:
13:       g.drawImage(image,
14:                      0, 0, r.width, r.height, this);
15:    }
16: }
```

In line 7, we get the image by using the applet `getImage` call. This method takes either an absolute URL or a URL and a name relative to the first URL. It actually doesn't fetch the image right away. Instead it records from where the image is to come and returns right away. When the image is first drawn to the screen, the actual fetching of the image occurs. This saves time and space if the image isn't drawn until needed. We use the relative URL version of `getImage` here and pass in the result of the Applet `getDocumentBase` method, which returns the URL that contains this applet. Thus the image name specified in line 8 is relative to the URL of the document that contains this applet.

In line 13 we call the version of the Graphics `drawImage` method that scales the image. All of the `drawImage` methods take an argument called an `ImageObserver`. This is an object that is told whenever there is incoming data for the image, so that the image can be drawn incrementally as it comes in over the wire. Luckily we don't have to worry about the details of how to do this. All we do is just pass in a pointer to the applet itself, because all applets can do incremental image drawing. Therefore we pass in `this` as the last argument to `drawImage`. Another useful feature of this method is that if you pass in a width and height as we do above, it'll automatically scale the image. Thus as the applet is resized, `drawImage` will scale the image to the new size before it's painted. See Figure 6.8.

MAKING YOUR APPLET CONFIGURABLE

At this point we've built three simple applets that can draw a line, a rectangle, or a centered string. However, the applets are not easily configured. For example, if someone wanted to change the color used in any of these three applets or the string that prints out in the centered string applet, they'd have to change the

Figure 6.8   drawImage applet

code for the applet. Most applet users aren't interested in writing applets (either because they're not programmers or they don't have the time), but they'd be willing to change attributes in existing applets if didn't involve coding.

In order to demonstrate how to make the applet more easily configured, we'll combine the three applets from the previous section into one applet that accepts the following attributes:

Shape
Shape of the image that's drawn by the applet. Can be one of the following: Line, Rectangle, String, or Image.

Color
Color in the foreground.

Text
String to draw if the Shape attribute is String.

Image
Image to draw if the Shape attribute is Image.

We'll also make the applet use a default if an attribute isn't specified. That way it can be included in an HTML file even if the user doesn't want to customize it.

Let's start by defining a method in our applet in which a color for the Color attribute is passed in as a string and turned into a Color object that we can use. To do this, we'll assume that the string is either a name of one of the predefined colors in the Color class or a number in hex (base 16) format. This number represents what is known as an *rgb* value, where "r" is the amount of red in the color, "g" the amount of green, and "b" is the amount of blue. Each rgb value is two letters in the string, which can go from 0 to ff (which is 255 in base 10). Here are some sample colors in hex format:

ff0000
red—maximum red value, with 0 for green and blue

00ff00
green

0000ff	blue
ffffff	white—maximum red, green, and blue values
000000	black
bbbbbb	light gray

Listing 6.6 shows the method we've just defined, which we'll call colorFrom-String, in action.

LISTING 6.6 colorFromString

```
1:   public Color colorFromString(String s,
2:                              Color defaultColor) {
3:     Integer i;
4:     try {
5:       i = Integer.valueOf(s, 16);
6:       return new Color(i.intValue());
7:     } catch (NumberFormatException e) {
8:       if (s.equalsIgnoreCase("red")) {
9:         return Color.red;
10:      } else if (s.equalsIgnoreCase("green")) {
11:        return Color.green;
12:      } else if (s.equalsIgnoreCase("blue")) {
13:        return Color.blue;
14:      } else if (s.equalsIgnoreCase("black")) {
15:        return Color.black;
16:      } else if (s.equalsIgnoreCase("white")) {
17:        return Color.white;
18:      } else {
19:        return defaultColor;
20:      }
21:    }
```

The method will return a default color if all else goes wrong (line 19). That way we can always specify a suitable default if the color string was illegal (another possibility is to indicate an error). In lines 5–6 we try to turn the string into a number using the static method Integer.valueOf, which takes a string and a base. If this method succeeds, then a new Color object is returned with the value of the integer. Otherwise, we'll get an exception. This tells us that the string really wasn't an integer, so we try to compare it against a few predetermined color names. If none of the comparisons succeed, we return the default color.

Next, we'll add some fields to hold the values we read in from the HTML tags:

```
public class GraphicsApplet extends Applet {
  Font appFont;
  Color appColor;
  String appShape;
  String appText;
  Image image;
```

Now we'll use the init method to get the values from the HTML parameters and turn them into real values. We can get the HTML parameters using the getParameter method, which will either return a string or null if the parameter wasn't specified in the HTML tag. We've coded Listing 6.7 to use suitable default values if a parameter wasn't specified.

LISTING 6.7 Getting HTML parameters

```
1:   public void init() {
2:       appFont = new Font("Helvetica",Font.BOLD,14);
3:       String arg = getParameter("COLOR");
4:       if (arg!= null) {
5:           appColor = colorFromString(arg,Color.red);
6:       }
7:       appShape = getParameter("SHAPE");
8:       if (appShape == null) {
9:           appShape = "Line";
10:      }
11:      appText = getParameter("TEXT");
12:      if (appText == null) {
13:          appText = "Graphics";
14:      }
15:      arg = getParameter("IMAGE");
16:      if (arg == null) {
17:          arg = "images/duke.gif";
18:      }
19:      image = getImage(getDocumentBase(), arg);
20:  }
```

Finally, Listing 6.8 shows our new paint method, which now takes into account the value of the appShape field when deciding which shape to draw:

LISTING 6.8 The new paint method

```
1:   public void paint(Graphics g) {
2:       Rectangle r = bounds();
3:       g.setColor(appColor);
4:       if (appShape.equalsIgnoreCase("line")) {
```

```
5:      g.drawLine(0, 0, r.width, r.height);
6:    } else if (appShape.equalsIgnoreCase(
7:                                     "rectangle")) {
8:      g.drawRect(0, 0, r.width - 1, r.height - 1);
9:    } else if (appShape.equalsIgnoreCase("image")) {
10:     g.drawImage(image,0,0,r.width,r.height,this);
11:   } else if(appShape.equalsIgnoreCase("string")){
12:     g.setFont(appFont);
13:     drawCenteredString(appText, g, r);
14:   }
15: }
```

Let's try out our configurable applet. Here is an HTML tag to pass in:

```
<title>GraphicsApplet</title>
<applet code="GraphicsApplet.class" width=200
  height=200>
  <param name=shape value="Line">
  <param name=color value="00ff00">
</applet>
```

This tag will configure the applet to draw a green line. See Figure 6.9. Now let's try drawing a rectangle instead. Here is the HTML tag:

```
<title>GraphicsApplet</title>
<applet code="GraphicsApplet.class" width=200
  height=200>
  <param name=shape value="Rectangle">
  <param name=color value="00ff00">
</applet>
```

FIGURE 6.9 Drawing a green line

FIGURE 6.10 Drawing a rectangle

The result is seen in Figure 6.10

Here's an HTML tag that will cause the applet to draw the string "Applets are forever" in purple:

```
<title>GraphicsApplet</title>
<applet code="GraphicsApplet.class" width=200
   height=200>
   <param name=shape value="String">
   <param name=color value="ff00ff">
   <param name=text value="Applets are forever">
</applet>
```

The result is shown in Figure 6.11.

FIGURE 6.11 Drawing a string

Finally, let's try an example that draws an image of the friendly HotJava mascot, Duke.

```
<title>GraphicsApplet</title>
<applet code="GraphicsApplet.class" width=200
  height=200>
  <param name=shape value="Image">
  <param name=image value="images/duke.gif">
</applet>
```

Refer back to Figure 6.8 to see the result.

ADDING UI CONTROLS

We saw in the section on "The Abstract Window Toolkit" on page 127 how to create some simple stand-alone UI applications with the AWT. Fortunately, it is equally simple to add UI controls to applets. The Applet class is really a subclass of the AWT Panel class, which contains and lays out embedded components. Let's begin our discussion with an applet that has a text field and a button. Whenever the button is pressed, the applet will display the current contents of the text field on the status line. See Listing 6.9.

LISTING 6.9 Applet with text field and button

```
 1:  import java.awt.*;
 2:  import java.applet.*;
 3:
 4:  public class UIApplet extends Applet {
 5:     TextField txt;
 6:     public void init() {
 7:        txt = new TextField(10);
 8:        add(txt);
 9:        add(new Button("Show"));
10:     }
11:     public boolean action(Event evt, Object arg) {
12:        showStatus(txt.getText());
13:        return true;
14:     }
15:  }
```

Figure 6.12 shows what this applet looks like when it runs.

FIGURE 6.12   Applet with a text field and button

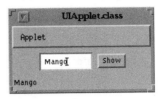

Note that the user typed "Mango" in the text field and that's what is shown on the status line. The code for this applet is relatively simple. In the init method, we add the UI controls using the add method, which is inherited from the AWT Container class. This method adds the AWT component to the given container, in this case the applet itself. In the AWT, every container can have the layout manager as an associated object, which is responsible for placing the components in an associated object called at initialization and whenever the container is invalidated either by resizing an associated object or by adding more components. In the case of the applet in Listing 6.9, it uses the default layout manager for applets which is the FlowLayout class. This class simply arranges the components from left to right and centers them horizontally.

The action method is inherited from the AWT Component class since it is the root of all (well, most) AWT objects. It's called whenever a component sends an action event. The component can either handle this event by default or it's propagated up the containment hierarchy. In this case, neither the text field or the button do anything to catch the event, so it gets caught by the applet's action method. Note that this method doesn't distinguish between the text field or the button, so it'll run either when the button is pressed or when the user hits return in the text field.

There are other layout classes available in the AWT. One of them, BorderLayout, can lay out five components according to their orientation: North, South, East, West, and Center. It places the components and then adjusts the size of the north and south components so their width is the maximum width. The east and west components are adjusted so their height is the maximum height, and the center component is given any vertical or horizontal space left over.

Since the layout manager needs to know what the orientation of each component is, we use a variant of the add method that takes a string as the first argument, which is the orientation of the component that is being added.

To illustrate this layout, let's write an applet that arranges five buttons with the BorderLayout class. See Listing 6.10.

LISTING 6.10 Laying out buttons by orientation

```
1:   import java.awt.*;
2:   import java.applet.*;
3:
4:   public class UIApplet extends Applet {
5:     public void init() {
6:       setLayout(new BorderLayout());
7:       setBackground(Color.red);
8:       setForeground(Color.white);
9:
10:       add("North", new Button("North"));
11:       add("South", new Button("South"));
12:       add("Center", new Button("Center"));
13:       add("West", new Button("West"));
14:       add("East", new Button("East"));
15:     }
16:     public boolean action(Event evt, Object arg) {
17:       showStatus(((Button)evt.target).getLabel());
18:       return true;
19:     }
20:   }
```

Figure 6.13 shows the result of running the applet in Listing 6.10.

Note that in the init method, the calls to set the foreground and background of the applet have the effect of being inherited by the AWT components contained in the applet. Thus all the buttons appear with a red background and white foreground.

FIGURE 6.13   Button orientation

You can get more complex layouts by using embedded panels. Each panel can have its own layout method to achieve different effects. To illustrate this concept, let's change the last applet slightly so that the center component is an embedded panel with another BorderLayout layout method. See Listing 6.11.

LISTING 6.11 **Using embedded panels**

```
 1:  import java.awt.*;
 2:  import java.applet.*;
 3:
 4:  public class UIApplet extends Applet {
 5:     public void init() {
 6:        setLayout(new BorderLayout());
 7:
 8:        setBackground(Color.red);
 9:        setForeground(Color.white);
10:
11:        add("North", new Button("North"));
12:        add("South", new Button("South"));
13:
14:        // create a recursive panel with buttons in it.
15:        Panel p = new Panel();
16:        p.setBackground(Color.lightGray);
17:        p.setLayout(new BorderLayout());
18:        add("Center", p);
19:        p.add("North", new Button("North"));
20:        p.add("South", new Button("South"));
21:        p.add("Center", new Button("Center"));
22:        p.add("West", new Button("West"));
23:        p.add("East", new Button("East"));
24:
25:        add("West", new Button("West"));
26:        add("East", new Button("East"));
27:     }
28:     public boolean action(Event evt, Object arg) {
29:       showStatus(((Button)evt.target).getLabel());
30:       return true;
31:     }
32:  }
```

Note that in lines 15–23 we add a Panel object that has five buttons arranged using another BorderLayout layout manager instead of adding a button as the center component. Figure 6.14 shows the resulting applet.

FIGURE **6.14**   Embedded panels

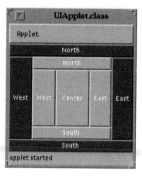

We've presented some simple examples that use AWT components inside of applets. Many more features are possible with the AWT, which you can explore by looking at some of the advanced examples on the CD-ROM.

ANIMATION

So far we have seen applets that respond to paint calls by drawing graphics on the screen. However, you probably would like to code animations that appear active on the screen to jazz up a static Web page. Although this might seem hard to program, it's actually very simple conceptually. With the support from the Java runtime, it's also simple in practice.

The basic idea behind animation is to present still images that are very similar in appearance but have slight variations in rapid succession to give the illusion of motion. The speed at which the images are presented is known as the *frame rate*. Here is pseudocode for doing an animation:

```
While (moreFramesToPaint) {
   paintCurrentFrame();
   sleep for some time; // determines the frame rate
   advanceToNextFrame();
}
```

The frame rate plays a crucial role in how the animation is perceived. If it's too slow, the animation will seem jumpy. However, if it's too fast, the viewer won't be able to perceive the transitions between the frames. Instead, only the last frame will be seen. This is the reason why the code sleeps between each frame. The speed of the frame rate is limited by how fast each frame can be painted on the screen, so anything that can be done to paint the frames efficiently will help improve the frame rate. We'll see a couple of simple techniques to make the animation seem smoother.

If we look at the animation pseudocode above, we see the sleep period will make everything stop until the time has elapsed. For an applet, this isn't a good thing, because it means that the paint method will block the other applets from being painted. The way to get around this is to use threads. The basic strategy is to create a thread that periodically wakes up (according to the desired speed of the animation) and tells the applet to repaint itself. This frees up the other applets to paint on the screen, and only when the next frame in the animation is required to be painted will the animation applet be called. Listing 6.12 shows the general pattern for an animation applet in Java.

LISTING 6.12 Code pattern for making an animation applet

```
1:  public class AnimationApplet extends Applet
2:                          implements Runnable {
3:      Thread animator;
4:
5:      public void init() {
6:          animator = new Thread(this);
7:      }
8:      public void start() {
9:          if (animator.isAlive()) {
10:             animator.resume();
11:         } else {
12:             animator.start();
13:         }
14:     }
15:     public void stop() {
16:         animator.suspend();
17:     }
18:     public void destroy() {
19:         animator.stop();
20:     }
21:     public void run() {
22:         while (true) {
23:             repaint();
24:             Thread.sleep(500); // sleep for some time
25:             // advance to the next frame
26:         }
27:     }
28:     public void paint(Graphics g) {
29:         // paint the current frame
30:     }
31: }
```

The run method in line 21 looks much like the animation pseudocode we presented earlier. The difference is that when the run method calls the sleep function, it only puts the animator thread to sleep, not the thread that is running the paint method. This allows the rest of the system to continue execution while the animation thread sleeps until it's time to paint the next frame.

Also, note that the lifecycle methods start, stop, and destroy modify the state of the animator thread appropriately. It's not good style to keep a thread running when the applet is not viewable (at least not when the thread is responsible for repainting the applet), so the stop method pauses the thread. Similarly, when an applet is destroyed, it should clean up any threads that it created.

Let's apply this pattern to a simple animation applet that takes a geometric shape, such as a line or a rectangle, and bounces it around the applet's display surface at random. To allow for extensibility later on, we'll structure the applet so that the code in Listing 6.12 drives the animation, but the actual animation is left to an Animation class that knows how to advance to the next frame and paint the current frame. Listing 6.13 shows this Animation class:

LISTING 6.13   A base class for animation

```
 1:  class Animation {
 2:     protected Applet app;
 3:     /** initialize this animation */
 4:     protected void init(Applet app) {
 5:        this.app = app;
 6:     }
 7:     /** advance to the next frame */
 8:     public abstract void advance();
 9:
10:     /** paint the current frame */
11:     public abstract void paintFrame(Graphics g);
12:  }
```

Let's create a subclass that picks a random set of coordinates in which to bounce a rectangle around (see Listing 6.14).

LISTING 6.14   An animation subclass that bounces a rectangle at random

```
 1:  class RectangleAnimation extends Animation {
 2:     private int cx = 0;
 3:     private int cy = 0;
 4:
 5:     /** pick random coordinates for the next frame */
 6:     public void advance() {
 7:        Rectangle bounds = app.bounds();
 8:        cx = (Math.random() * 1000) % bounds.width;
 9:        cy = (Math.random() * 1000) % bounds.height;
10:     }
```

```
11:     /** paint a rectangle at the current coordinates */
12:     public void paintFrame(Graphics g) {
13:        g.setColor(Color.blue);
14:        g.drawRect(cx, cy, 50, 50);
15:     }
16: }
```

Now we can plug this class into the animation pattern above and get an animation applet of a bouncing rectangle, Listing 6.15.

LISTING 6.15 An animation applet that bounces a rectangle at random

```
1:  public class AnimationApplet extends Applet
2:                          implements Runnable {
3:     Thread animator;
4:     Animation animation;
5:
6:     public void init() {
7:        animator = new Thread(this);
8:        animation = new RectangleAnimation();
9:        animation.init(this);
10:    }
11:    public void start() {
12:       if (animator.isAlive()) {
13:          animator.resume();
14:       } else {
15:          animator.start();
16:       }
17:    }
18:    public void stop() {
19:       animator.suspend();
20:    }
21:    public void destroy() {
22:       animator.stop();
23:    }
24:    public void run() {
25:       while (true) {
26:          repaint();
27:          Thread.sleep(500); // sleep for some time
28:          animation.advance();
29:       }
30:    }
31:    public void paint(Graphics g) {
32:       animation.paintFrame(g);
33:    }
34: }
```

One obvious way to change this applet would be to make it configurable in the same way that we did with the graphics applet at the beginning of the chapter. However, a more interesting way to make this applet configurable is to make the subclass used for the animation a parameter. Rather than hard-wire in the applet which animation subclasses it knows, we'll just pass in the name of the subclass as a parameter and use that name to create an instance of the animation. The Java applet runtime will take care of loading the code if necessary. This allows new animation subclasses to be written and just dropped into the same directory that contains the applet. Web pages that want to make use of the new animation only need to pass in the name of the new subclass rather then recompile the applet with the new subclass.

Listing 6.16 shows the new version of the init method that allows this customization.

LISTING 6.16   Making the applet configurable with the name of a subclass to load

```
1:    public void init() {
2:        animator = new Thread(this);
3:        String subclassName = getParameter("animation");
4:        animation =
5:            Class.forName(subclassName).newInstance();
6:        animation.init(this);
7:    }
```

The call in line 5 causes the Java runtime to allocate an object given the class name. If this class name isn't currently found, the runtime will load the class over the net from the same place as the applet.

This is the corresponding HTML tag that would be used to tell this animation applet to use the RectangleAnimation subclass shown above in Listing 6.16:

```
<applet code=AnimationApplet.class height=300 width=300>
<param name=animation value="RectangleAnimation">
</applet>
```

A useful technique when doing animation is using what is known as *double-buffering* to make the animation seem smoother. The basic idea behind this technique is to paint the applet into an offscreen image (an image that isn't displayed to the screen). When that is done, then the entire image is painted to the screen once. Often this can make a dramatic improvement in the quality of the animation since the intermediate steps in the paint process aren't shown. This code snippet shows the basic mechanism for setting up a Graphics object that paints into an offscreen image. You can then use the drawImage call to paint the offscreen image to the screen:

```
Image offscreenImage = createImage(width, height);
Graphics offscreenGfx = offscreenImage.getGraphics();
```

You can do something like this in your applet's `init` method by creating the image and graphics objects fields and use them in your `paint` method.

Another trick that's useful for doing animation is to define an `update` method on your applet. This method is called when your applet issues a repaint call (by default `update` calls `paint`). The advantage is that you can separate your methods into a `paint` method that always paints everything and an `update` method that can assume the background is painted so it only paints what has changed.

FUTURE PROJECT IDEAS

Now that you've seen some examples of how to write an applet, it's time for you to write some on your own. To get you started, here are some ideas, ordered from easier to more difficult, for applets you could build. There's no better way to learn this stuff than by just diving in. It's true that not all of the API was covered in these chapters. But by looking at the documentation in the CD-ROM and experimenting with some of the applets, you should soon be comfortable with the rest of the API.

So here are some ideas:

▶ Experiment with the graphics primitives. For example, add a new shape to the configurable graphics applet presented above to draw a polygon and a circle. Add a parameter to the applet to control whether the shape should be filled or not.

▶ Add a mode to the graphics applet so that it centers the image as unscaled rather than scaling the image to the size of the applet.

▶ Add a mode to the graphics applet so that it tiles the image across the entire applet.

▶ Use a text field and the `showDocument` call to make a simple applet that lets you type in an URL and visit it when you hit Return (this will only work inside a Web browser).

▶ Learn about the AWT `List` component that lets you put up a list of strings. Make an applet that takes a list of URLs and builds a scrolling list with them. When you select one of the items in the list, use `showDocument` to visit that URL.

▶ Use subpanels to change the graphics applet so that there are buttons at the bottom that let the user change which shape is painted. You'll need to make a `panel` subclass to paint the shape and another panel to hold the buttons.

▶ Change the Animation class presented in the last section by adding an Animation class that takes a list of points and animates the shape by drawing it, starting at each point in the list. When it hits the end of the list, it starts over.

▶ When you've done the previous project, extend the path animation by letting the user enter the points with the mouse. Make two buttons, one to reset the path to null and another to restart the animation with the current path.

▶ Work on making the Animation applet more configurable. For example, when it sleeps for 500 milliseconds, make that into a parameter.

If you want more examples, visit the Java/HotJava site at:

 http://www.javasoft.com/

and follow the links to the various Java applets. All of the applets there that were written at Sun, as well as many that weren't, have the source code available, so it's an excellent way to learn more about applet programming.

Have fun!

Applet Guide

This Appendix is a quick-reference guide to all the applets covered in this book that are on the CD-ROM. It should prove to be handy when you're looking for an applet that has a particular behavior, such as animation or audio effects.

Applet Name	Animation	Audio	Graphics	Mouse	Keyboard	Text Tricks	See Page
Abacus			■	■			46
Animator	■	■		■			47
AudioItem		■					49
Ballistic Simulator	■	■	■	■			50
Bar Chart				■			51
Bar Graph				■	■		53
Blinking Text	■					■	56
Bouncing Heads	■	■					57
Clock	■			■			58
Crossword Puzzle			■	■	■	■	59
Dining Philosophers	■	■		■			60
Escher Paint			■	■	■		61
Graph Layout	■		■	■			62
ImageLoop	■			■			64
ImageMap	■	■	■	■			65
LED Sign	■					■	68

Applet Name	Animation	Audio	Graphics	Mouse	Keyboard	Text Tricks	See Page
Line Graph			■	■			70
Link Button		■		■			72
Molecule Viewer			■	■			73
Neon Sign	■						75
Nervous Text	■					■	76
Nuclear Powerplant	■	■	■	■			77
Pythagoras' Theorem	■		■	■		■	78
Scrolling Images	■						79
SpreadSheet			■	■	■		81
Tic-Tac-Toe		■		■			83
Tumbling Duke	■						84
Under Construction	■	■					85
Voltage Circuit Simulator		■		■			86
What's New!	■						87
Wire Frame Viewer			■	■			88
Zine			■	■		■	90

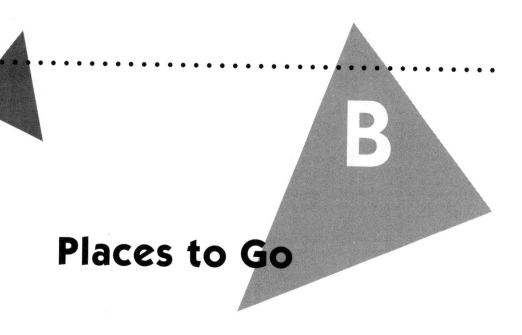

Places to Go

Throughout *Hooked on Java*, we've listed URLs for World-Wide Web sites where you can get more information on a variety of topics related to Java. To make things even easier, we've filled this appendix with a number of vital URLs—some that you've seen before in this book and some not. These are links that will further your knowledge of Java and the Internet, and we're sure you'll want to add them to your lists of favorite sites.

 http://www.javasoft.com/hooked/

We created these Web pages expressly for you, our readers. Here you'll find copious links to interesting places that are relevant to Java, as well as the latest scoop on the applets that are covered in this book. Updates, corrections, and other good stuff will be included here.

 http://www.javasoft.com/

Want to get the most up-to-date information on Java, Java applets, and HotJava? Visit Sun Microsystems' Java/HotJava home page. And visit frequently, if you want to stay in touch with what's going on in Java land.

 http://www.javasoft.com/applets/

Links to scads and scads of Java applets and Java-powered pages can be found at this tasty site. It's an excellent place to get inspiration for creating your own Java-powered pages.

news:comp.lang.java

This Internet newsgroup is a fount of information for Java programming language issues. Check it out if you have questions about Java and Java applets.

mailto:java@java.sun.com

Send inquiries about Java, Java applets, and HotJava directly to this e-mail address. It's probably the quickest way to get help from Sun Microsystems.

http://www.sun.com/

Visit the Sun Microsystems home page for the latest details on Sun products and support information.

http://www.gamelan.com/

This archive of Java resources is a great place to find Java applets, Java libraries, and other Java programming tools.

http://www.io.org/~mentor/DigitalEspresso.html

This Web site has a summary of the traffic on the Java mailing lists and newsgroups. You'll find concise information on the Java issues that people are talking about.

http://www.netscape.com/

Naturally, Netscape Communications Inc.'s home page is the best source of up-to-date information on Java support in Netscape Navigator.

http://www.yahoo.com/

If you're looking for information on a specific topic, visit Yahoo. It lets you quickly search through millions of Web pages to find what you need. Come here when you're lost.

http://www.dimensionx.com/

We've found this to be a good source of Java applets and information on Java.

http://www.w3.org/

The home page for the World Wide Web Consortium is an excellent starting point for finding information on the World-Wide Web, HTML, protocols, browsers, etc.

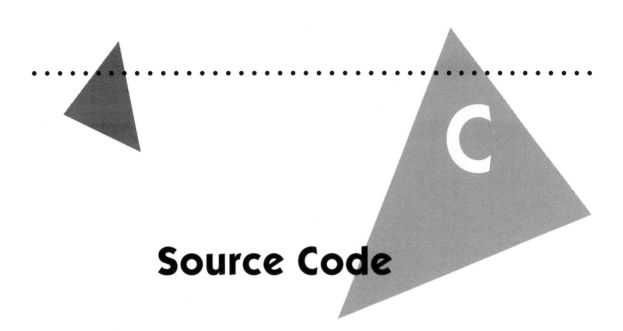

Source Code

For easy reference, the source code for the applets that were presented in Chapter 6, "Building an Applet," is listed in this appendix.

BUILDING AN APPLET

Listing C.1 is the source code for the configurable GraphicsApplet presented on page 138.

LISTING C.1   GraphicsApplet

```
 1:  /*
 2:   * GraphicsApplet
 3:   *
 4:   * An applet that draws different shapes depending
 5:   * on the configuration of the HTML tag. It
 6:   * accepts the following attributes in addition
 7:   * to the standard attributes:
 8:   *
 9:   *    SHAPE - one of "Line","Rectangle","String"
10:   *           or "Image"
11:   *    COLOR - which foreground color to use.
12:   *    TEXT - If SHAPE is "String" this is the
13:   *           text to draw.
14:   *    IMAGE - If SHAPE is "Image" this is the
15:   *            image to draw.
16:   */
17:  import java.awt.*;
18:  import java.applet.*;
```

```
19:   public class GraphicsApplet extends Applet {
20:     /** which font to use for string drawing.*/
21:     Font   appFont;
22:
23:     /** which foreground color to use */
24:     Color  appColor;
25:
26:     /** which type of shape to draw. */
27:     String appShape;
28:
29:     /** which text to draw if appShape is "String"*/
30:     String appText;
31:
32:     /** which image to draw if appShape is "Image"*/
33:     Image  image;
34:
35:     /**
36:      * Initialize the applet. Set the fields above
37:      * according to the parameters in the HTML tags
38:      * or use suitable defaults if the parameter
39:      * isn't specified.
40:      */
41:     public void init() {
42:       appFont = new Font("Helvetica",Font.BOLD,14);
43:       String arg = getParameter("COLOR");
44:       if (arg != null) {
45:         appColor = colorFromString(arg,Color.red);
46:       }
47:       appShape = getParameter("SHAPE");
48:       if (appShape == null) {
49:         appShape = "Line";
50:       }
51:       appText = getParameter("TEXT");
52:       if (appText == null) {
53:         appText = "Graphics";
54:       }
55:       arg = getParameter("image");
56:       if (arg != null) {
57:         image = getImage(getDocumentBase(), arg);
58:       }
59:     }
60:
61:
62:     /**
63:      * Reads a color description from s and returns
64:      * a Color object that matches the description.
65:      * If the description isn't valid then this
66:      * method returns defaultColor.
```

```
67:      * The description s can be either the strings
68:      * "red","green", "blue","black","white" or
69:      * a number in hex that represents the rgb
70:      * value of the desired color.
71:      */
72:     public Color colorFromString(String s,
73:                                   Color defaultColor) {
74:        Integer i;
75:
76:        try {
77:          i = Integer.valueOf(s, 16);
78:          return new Color(i.intValue());
79:        } catch (NumberFormatException e) {
80:          return defaultColor;
81:        }
82:     }
83:
84:
85:     /**
86:      * Draws a string s centered in the rectangle
87:      * r. The given Graphics object g is used to
88:      * do the actual drawing.
89:      */
90:     public void drawCenteredString(String s,
91:                                    Graphics g,
92:                                    Rectangle r) {
93:        FontMetrics fm = g.getFontMetrics(appFont);
94:
95:        g.drawString(s,
96:          (r.width - fm.stringWidth(s))/2,
97:          (r.height - fm.getHeight()) / 2);
98:     }
99:
100:    /**
101:     * This method is called when the applet
102:     * needs to be redrawn. It basically looks at
103:     * appShape to determine which shape needs to
104:     * be drawn.
105:     */
106:    public void paint(Graphics g) {
107:       Dimension r = size();
108:
109:       g.setColor(appColor);
110:       if (appShape.equalsIgnoreCase("line")) {
111:         g.drawLine(0, 0, r.width, r.height);
112:       } else if (appShape.
113:             equalsIgnoreCase("rectangle")) {
114:         g.drawRect(0,0,r.width - 1, r.height - 1);
```

```
115:        } else if(appShape.equalsIgnoreCase("image")) {
116:            g.drawImage(image,0,0,r.width,r.height,this);
117:        } else if (appShape.
118:                        equalsIgnoreCase("string")) {
119:        g.setFont(appFont);
120:        drawCenteredString(appText, g, r);
121:        }
122:    }
123: }
```

Listing C.2 is an example of an applet with UI controls, which was accomplished by using an embedded panel in the source code. It was presented on page 144.

LISTING C.2 Applet with UI controls

```
1:  import java.awt.*;
2:  import java.applet.*;
3:
4:  public class UIApplet extends Applet {
5:    public void init() {
6:        setLayout(new BorderLayout());
7:
8:        setBackground(Color.red);
9:        setForeground(Color.white);
10:
11:       add("North", new Button("North"));
12:       add("South", new Button("South"));
13:
14:       // create a recursive panel with buttons in it.
15:       Panel p = new Panel();
16:       p.setBackground(Color.lightGray);
17:       p.setLayout(new BorderLayout());
18:       add("Center", p);
19:       p.add("North", new Button("North"));
20:       p.add("South", new Button("South"));
21:       p.add("Center", new Button("Center"));
22:       p.add("West", new Button("West"));
23:       p.add("East", new Button("East"));
24:
25:       add("West", new Button("West"));
26:       add("East", new Button("East"));
27:    }
28:    public boolean action(Event evt, Object arg) {
29:      showStatus(((Button)evt.target).getLabel());
30:      return true;
31:    }
32: }
```

Listing C.3 is the source code for the animation applet that was presented on page 148:

LISTING C.3 Code pattern for making an animation applet

```
 1:  public class AnimationApplet extends Applet
 2:                       implements Runnable {
 3:    Thread animator;
 4:    Animation animation;
 5:
 6:    public void init() {
 7:      animator = new Thread(this);
 8:      String name = getParameter("animation");
 9:      if (name == null) {
10:        name = "RectangleAnimation";
11:      }
12:      // this call allocates an object of the type
13:      // given. If necessary, the code will be loaded
14:      // over the net
15:      animation = Class.forName(name).newInstance();
16:      animation.init(this);
17:    }
18:    public void start() {
19:      if (animator.isAlive()) {
20:        animator.resume();
21:      } else {
22:        animator.start();
23:      }
24:    }
25:    public void stop() {
26:      animator.suspend();
27:    }
28:    public void destroy() {
29:      animator.stop();
30:    }
31:    public void run() {
32:      while (true) {
33:        repaint();
34:        Thread.sleep(500); // sleep for some time
35:        animation.advance();
36:      }
37:    }
38:    public void paint(Graphics g) {
39:      animation.paintFrame(g);
40:    }
41:  }
42:
43:  /**
```

```
44:    * A base class for animation types.
45:    */
46:   class Animation {
47:     protected Applet app;
48:     /** initialize this animation */
49:     protected void init(Applet app) {
50:        this.app = app;
51:     }
52:     /** advance to the next frame */
53:     public abstract void advance();
54:
55:     /** paint the current frame */
56:     public abstract void paintFrame(Graphics g);
57:   }
58:
59:   /**
60:    * An example animation that bounces a rectangle
61:    * at random on the screen.
62:    */
63:   class RectangleAnimation extends Animation {
64:     private int cx = 0;
65:     private int cy = 0;
66:
67:     /** pick random coordinates for the next frame */
68:     public void advance() {
69:        Rectangle bounds = app.bounds();
70:        cx = (Math.random() * 1000) % bounds.width;
71:        cy = (Math.random() * 1000) % bounds.height;
72:     }
73:     /** paint a rectangle at the current coordinates */
74:     public void paintFrame(Graphics g) {
75:        g.setColor(Color.blue);
76:        g.drawRect(cx, cy, 50, 50);
77:     }
78:   }
```

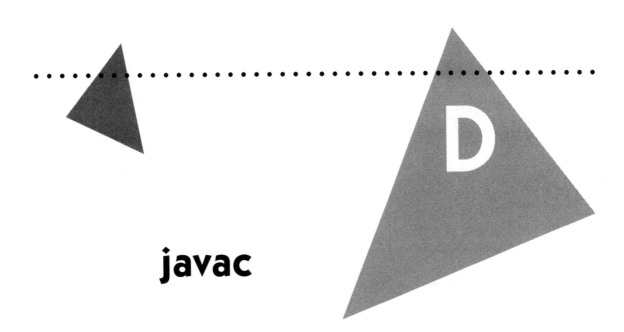

javac

This appendix contains the man pages for the Java compiler.

Command

javac—the Java compiler. The javac command compiles Java programs.

Synopsis

```
javac [ options ] filename.java ...
javac_g [ options ] filename.java ...
```

Description

The javac command compiles Java source code into Java byte-codes. You then use the Java interpreter—the java command—to interpret the Java byte-codes.

Java source code must be contained in files whose filenames end with the .java extension. For every class defined in the source files passed to javac, the compiler stores the resulting byte-codes in a file named classname.class. The compiler places the resulting .class files in the same directory as the corresponding .java file (unless you specify the -d option).

When you define your own classes, you need to specify their location. Use CLASSPATH to do this. CLASSPATH consists of a semi-colon-separated list of directories that specifies the path. If the source files passed to javac reference a class not defined in any of the other files passed to javac, then javac searches for the referenced class using the class path. For example:

```
.;\users\dac\classes
```

Note that the system always appends the location of the system classes onto the end of the class path, unless you use the -classpath option to specify a path.

javac_g is a non-optimized version of javac suitable for use with debuggers like jdb.

Options

-classpath path

Specifies the path javac uses to look up classes. Overrides the default or the CLASSPATH environment variable if it is set. Directories are separated by semicolons. Thus the general format for path is:

```
.;<your_path>
```

For example:

```
.;\users\avh\classes;\jdk\classes
```

-d directory

Specifies the root directory of the class hierarchy. Thus, doing:

```
javac -d <my_dir> MyProgram.java
```

causes the .class files for the classes in the MyProgram.java source file to be saved in the directory my_dir.

-g

Enables generation of debugging tables. Debugging tables contain information about line numbers and local variables—information used by Java debugging tools. By default, only line numbers are generated, unless optimization (-O) is turned on.

-nowarn

Turns off warnings. If used, the compiler does not print out any warnings.

-O

Optimizes compiled code by inlining static, final, and private methods. Note that your classes may get larger in size.

-verbose

Causes the compiler and linker to print out messages about what source files are being compiled and what class files are being loaded.

Environment

CLASSPATH   Used to provide the system a path to user-defined classes. Directories are separated by colons. For example:

```
.:/home/avh/classes:/usr/local/java/classes
```

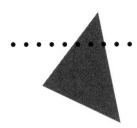

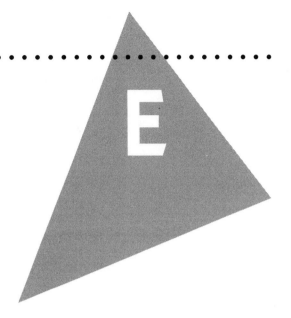

java

This appendix contains the man pages for the Java interpreter.

Command

java—the Java interpreter. java interprets (executes) Java byte-codes.

Synopsis

```
java [ options ] classname <args>
java_g [ options ] classname <args>
```

Description

The java command executes Java byte-codes created by javac, the Java compiler.

The classname argument is the name of the class to be executed. classname must be fully qualified by including its package in the name. For example:

```
java java.lang.String
```

Note that any arguments that appear after classname on the command line are passed to the class's main() method.

java expects the byte-codes for the class to be in a file called classname.class, which is generated by compiling the corresponding source file with javac. All Java byte-code files end with the filename extension .class, which the compiler automatically adds when the class is compiled. `classname` must contain a `main()` method, defined as follows:

```
class Aclass {
  public static void main(String argv[]){
    ...
  }
}
```

`java` executes the `main()` method and then exits unless `main()` creates one or more threads. If any threads are created by `main()` , then `java` doesn't exit until the last thread exits.

When you define your own classes, you need to specify their location. Use `CLASSPATH` to do this. `CLASSPATH` consists of a semicolon-separated list of directories that specifies the path. For example:

```
.;C:\users\avh\classes
```

Note that the system always appends the location of the system classes onto the end of the class path, unless you use the `-classpath` option to specify a path.

Ordinarily, you compile source files with `javac`, then run the program using `java`. However, `java` can be used to compile and run programs when the `-cs` option is used. As each class is loaded, its modification date is compared to the modification date of the class source file. If the source has been modified more recently, it is recompiled and the new byte-code file is loaded. `java` repeats this procedure until all the classes are correctly compiled and loaded.

The interpreter can determine whether a class is legitimate through the mechanism of verification. Verification ensures that the byte-codes that are being interpreted do not violate any language constraints.

`java_g` is a non-optimized version of `java`, suitable for use with debuggers like `jdb`.

Options

-debug   Allows the Java debugger `jdb` to attach itself to this `java` session. When -debug is specified on the command line, `java` displays a password, which must be used when starting the debugging session.

-cs,   Causes the modification time of the class byte-code file to be
-checksource   compared to that of the class source file when a compiled class is loaded. If the source has been modified more recently, it is recompiled and the new byte-code file is loaded.

-classpath path	Specifies the path java uses to look up classes. Overrides the default or the CLASSPATH environment variable if it is set. Directories are separated by semicolons. Thus the general format for path is:

`.;<your_path>`

For example:

`.;C:\users\avh\classes;C:\jdk\classes`

-mx x	Sets the maximum size of the memory allocation pool (the garbage-collected heap) to x. The default is 16 megabytes of memory. x must be >1000 bytes.

    By default, x is measured in bytes. You can specify x in either kilobytes or megabytes by appending the letter k for kilobytes or the letter m for megabytes.

-ms x	Sets the startup size of the memory allocation pool (the garbage collected heap) to x. The default is 1 megabyte of memory. x must be >1000 bytes.

    By default, x is measured in bytes. You can specify x in either kilobytes or megabytes by appending the letter k for kilobytes or the letter m for megabytes.

-noasyncgc	Turns off asynchronous garbage collection. When activated, no garbage collection takes place unless it is explicitly called or the program runs out of memory. Normally, garbage collection runs as an asynchronous thread in parallel with other threads.

-ss x	Each java thread has two stacks: one for java code and one for C code. The -ss option sets the maximum stack size that can be used by C code in a thread to x. Every thread that is spawned during the execution of the program passed to java has x as its C stack size. The default units for x are bytes. x must be >1000 bytes.

    You can modify the meaning of x by appending either the letter k for kilobytes or the letter m for megabytes. The default stack size is 128 kilobytes (-ss 128k).

-oss x	Each java thread has two stacks: one for java code and one for C code. The -oss option sets the maximum stack size that can be used by java code in a thread to x. Every thread that is spawned

during the execution of the program passed to java has x as its java stack size. The default units for x are bytes. x must be >1000 bytes.

You can modify the meaning of x by appending either the letter k for kilobytes or the letter m for megabytes. The default stack size is 400 kilobytes (-oss 400k).

-t	Prints a trace of the instructions executed (java_g only).
-v, -verbose	Causes java to print a message to stdout each time a class file is loaded.
-verify	Runs the verifier on all code.
-verify remote	Runs the verifier on all code that is loaded into the system via a classloader. verifyremote is the default for the interpreter.
-noverify	Turns verification off.
-verbosegc	Causes the garbage collector to print out messages whenever it frees memory.
-Dproperty Name= newValue	Redefines a property value. propertyName is the name of the property whose value you want to change and newValue is the value to change it to. For example, this command line

```
java -Dawt.button.color=green ...
```

sets the value of the property awt.button.color to green. java accepts any number of -D options on the command line.

Environment

CLASSPATH	Used to provide the system a path to user-defined classes. Directories are separated by semicolons. For example:

```
.;C:\users\avh\classes;C:\jdk\classes
```

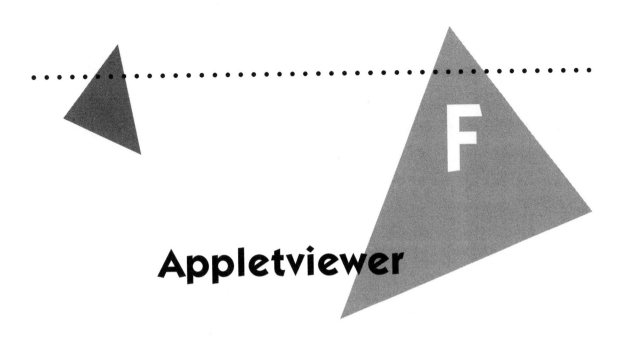

Appletviewer

This appendix contains the man pages for the Java Appletviewer.

Command

`appletviewer`—the Java Appletviewer. The `appletviewer` command allows you to run applets outside of the context of a World-Wide Web browser.

Synopsis

`appletviewer` [options] urls ...

Description

The `appletviewer` command connects to the document(s) or resource(s) designated by the URL(s) and displays each applet referenced by that document in its own window. Note: if the document(s) referred to by the URL(s) does not reference any applets with the `<applet>` tag, `appletviewer` does nothing.

Option

-debug   Starts the Appletviewer in the Java debugger `jdb`, thus allowing you to debug the applets in the document.

Applet
Tag Definition

This appendix contains the DTD[1] for the Java applet tag, which is supported by Netscape Navigator 2.0 and HotJava. Future Java-compatible browsers will also need to adhere to it.

```
<!ELEMENT APPLET - - (PARAM*, (%text;)*)>
<!ATTLIST APPLET
  CODEBASE CDATA #IMPLIED  -- code base --
  CODE CDATA #REQUIRED     -- code file --
  NAME CDATA #IMPLIED      -- applet name --
  WIDTH NUMBER #REQUIRED
  HEIGHT NUMBER #REQUIRED
  ALIGN (left|right|top|texttop|middle|
    absmiddle|baseline|bottom|absbottom) baseline
  VSPACE NUMBER #IMPLIED
  HSPACE NUMBER #IMPLIED
>
<!ELEMENT PARAM - O EMPTY>
<!ATTLIST PARAM
  NAME NAME #REQUIRED   -- The name of the parameter --
  VALUE CDATA #IMPLIED -- The value of the parameter --
>
```

Applet resources (including their classes) are normally loaded relative to the document-URL (or <base> tag if it is defined). The codebase attribute is used to

---

[1] Document Type Definition

change this default behavior. If the codebase attribute is defined, then it specifies a different location to find applet resources. The value can be an absolute URL or a relative URL. The absolute URL is used as is without modification and is not affected by the document's <base> tag. When the codebase attribute is relative, then it is relative to the document URL (or <base> tag if defined).

Here is an example:

```
<applet codebase="applets/NervousText"
  code=NervousText.class
  width=300
  height=50>
<param name=text value="Java is Cool!">
</applet>
```

Data from the applet tag (code, codebase, name, width, height, align, vspace, and hspace) is made available to the applet. In addition, any parameters defined in the <param> tags are also made available to the applet. The applet invokes the getParameter method to get a string that contains the value of one of the above parameters.

Applet resources are loaded relative to the codebase, including images, audio files, etc. However, the applet does have access to the document URL if resources from that location are desired.

Here is an example of how applet code can reference a resource from the codebase (this should be used when resources are accessed that are referenced directly from within the applet code):

```
Image img = getImage(new URL(getBaseURL(),
            "images/cross.gif"));
```

What follows is an example of how applet code can reference a resource from the document URL (this should be used when resources are accessed that are specified in an applet parameter, and which are therefore relative to the document's base):

```
Image img = getImage(new URL(getDocumentURL(),
            getParameter("src")));
```

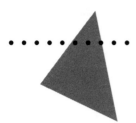

Index